# CHORES
# WITHOUT WARS

# CHORES WITHOUT WARS

*Turning Housework into Teamwork*

## NEW EDITION

## LYNN LOTT
## AND RIKI INTNER

TAYLOR TRADE PUBLISHING
Lanham • New York • Dallas • Boulder • Toronto • Oxford

Previous editions published in 1995 under the title *The Family That Works Together* . . . and in 1997 under the title *Chores without Wars*.

First Taylor Trade Publishing edition 2005

This Taylor Trade Publishing paperback edition of *Chores without Wars* is an original publication. It is published by arrangement with the authors.

Published by Taylor Trade Publishing
An imprint of The Rowman & Littlefield Publishing Group, Inc.
4501 Forbes Boulevard, Suite 200
Lanham, Maryland 20706

Distributed by National Book Network

**Library of Congress Cataloging-in-Publication Data**

Lott, Lynn.
   Chores without wars : turning housework into teamwork / Lynn Lott and Riki Intner.— New ed., 1st Taylor Trade Pub. ed.
      p. cm.
   Includes bibliographical references and index.
   ISBN 1-58979-262-9 (pbk. : alk. paper)
   1. Parenting—United States. 2. Family—United States. 3. Home economics—United States. I. Intner, Riki. II. Title.
   HQ755.8.L6764 2005
   646.7'8—dc22                                                    2005002642

♾™   The paper used in this publication meets the minimum requirements of American National Standard for Information Sciences—Permanence of Paper for Printed Library Materials, ANSI/NISO Z39.48–1992.
Manufactured in the United States of America.

# CONTENTS

# CONTENTS

# FOREWORD

When it comes to getting your children to do chores, do you ever say, "It is easier just to do it myself!"? This is usually followed by a "but": "But I know it is important for my children to learn responsibility and cooperation."

That latter statement is true; children do need to learn responsibility and cooperation and, with the help of this book, you'll find it *isn't* easier to do chores yourself. Get ready for a rest. Soon you'll have every member of your family (yes, husbands, too), joyfully (well, maybe just willingly) pitching in to help with all the household chores, jobs, duties, or whatever else you want to call what it takes to keep your home running smoothly.

Teamwork is a big deal in the corporate world—everyone wants to be an important, useful, contributing member of the team. It is the best way to be successful. You can create an atmosphere in your home where your children and spouse will see the value of family teamwork—and will want to be a usefully contributing member of the family team.

How, you may ask? Well, first you have to go to coaching school—found in this book. In *Chores without Wars* you'll learn how to develop an attitude that is encouraging and motivating. You'll learn skills that are encouraging and motivating. You'll learn to see every challenge as an opportunity for learning—for everyone in the family. You'll learn how to coach your family right into the *Chores without Wars* Olympics.

Will everything be perfect? Not unless you are a saint, your husband is a saint, and all your children are saints. You'll have lots of challenges. (Oh goody, more opportunities for learning!) And you'll have lots of skills to handle every challenge.

Have you ever wondered, "How can I be the very best parent I can be?" After reading *Chores without Wars*, not only will you end chore wars but along the way you'll also learn how to be the very best parent you can be.

Enjoy!

—JANE NELSEN

# ACKNOWLEDGMENTS

Thanks to all the families who shared problems and stories with us over the years so that our book could be practical and realistic. We send special love to our kids, stepkids, and now, grandchildren, who remind us every day of the fun and satisfaction that comes from families working together. We especially appreciate the efforts of our agent, June Clark, who took the "chore" out of finding the right home for this extremely helpful book.

# INTRODUCTION

## TAKING THE WAR OUT OF CHORES

When we tell people we are writing a book called *Chores without Wars*, we hear three responses. The first and most common is, "I could sure use that book. Let me know when it's done."

The second response is, "That's impossible! How can there be chores unless there are wars? My kids won't do anything unless I nag, threaten, or coerce them."

The third response is the most surprising. People ask us, "When are children old enough to help with chores?" When we give them our answer, they either shake their heads in agreement, or respond as the program director of a group of young parents did. We were discussing doing a workshop for her parenting group and suggested the topic Chores without Wars. We explained that this program had two goals. The first was to help parents involve kids in the tasks that keep a household running smoothly. The second was to show parents how chores are a medium through which we can teach respect, resourcefulness, responsibility, organizational skills, and shared decision making. Much to our surprise, her response was, "Oh, no, our children are too young for that." We asked how old the children were, and she replied, "They range from preschool to third grade."

This thinking is a common mistake many parents make. When children are two or three years old and anxious to "help," to push the vacuum or wash the tub, parents often scoot them off to play. The message is, "Stay out of the way so I can get this done quickly."

Years later when those same parents start looking for help with messy rooms, dirty dishes, and un-mowed lawns, they discover that their children have heeded their lesson too well and learned to stay out of the way when it comes to doing chores. Now they have to deal with reluctant helpers who wonder, "Why is she asking me to do this?"

*Chores without Wars* can save you this grief while helping empower your children. The book offers suggestions to make things work better for everyone in your home, whether there are two or ten of you. Families who have benefited from these ideas say that their children get up to their alarm clocks, clean their rooms, get ready for school, and make their own lunches without one little reminder. They also say that dads who were uninvolved before now pitch in naturally and happily. They walk the dog, feed the cat, take turns cooking and doing dishes, help with laundry, and sweep the floor.

Single parents benefit from these ideas, too. A dad who did everything himself when his sons came to stay now leaves a list of chores for his boys to complete before he gets home from work. His kids suggested this method. It was also their idea to choose items from the list and to do them on their own time schedule. They agreed that if their chores weren't done before Dad got home, they would do them immediately if he had to remind them, and they do. Prior to using the methods in this book, this father was angry and exhausted and disappointed in his sons. Now he feels more relaxed and has more time for himself and time to play with the boys.

*Chores without Wars* also works with busy families whose kids are running in all directions. A family of six whose four children were all involved in sports programs found that leaving lists was hopeless because no one was ever home to complete the chores on the list. When the parents scolded and criticized, the children rebelled, saying they were too busy with practices and games to help. When Mom and Dad asked the children to help figure out a way to get work done that was fair for the family, the kids responded with great ideas. No one in the family thought it was fair for only one person to do all the work. The children knew intimately about teamwork and fair play from their athletic experiences. They were willing to help the family if they could find jobs that didn't need to be done daily. The family brainstormed a list of possibilities and all the kids chipped in.

The methods are extremely helpful with stepfamilies. A household with six children of the his, hers, and ours variety struggled to come up with a plan that worked for children who weren't at the house on the same days. Assigning chores, making lists, and holding family meetings did not work. One day, in desperation, Mom took out a lunch bag and decorated the front with these words, "Look inside for ways to help the family and pick two." Then she filled the bag with chore suggestions on separate slips of paper, set the bag on the kitchen table, and went about her business. The youngest children were the most curious and soon pulled slips from the bag. They couldn't read so they found a parent or older sibling to tell them what was on the paper. This prompted Mom to add pictures to the slips along with the words. Soon everyone was pulling slips out of the bag, looking for something he or she liked doing. Amazingly, this simple system worked for several years, replacing the aggravation of trying to figure out a new plan every time a different configuration of kids showed up.

We've been teaching these ideas to families since the late seventies. The stories in this book are real, based on the trials and successes of families who've worked with *Chores without Wars*. Some of these families have sophisticated systems for chores. Others have less formal procedures. Some of the families are stepfamilies, some are single-parent households. Some families have a wide age range of children while others have an only child. No matter how many different family configurations we've worked with, what is true for all of them is that they've replaced chaos with friendly cooperation and have raised extremely capable children.

How did this happen? There's no secret. The parents wanted to do things differently and were willing to find a system that worked and then take the time to implement it. If you are one of those parents, this revised edition of *Chores without Wars* is filled with helpful information designed for you and your family. We know you are busy and pulled in many directions, so we've made this book as user-friendly as possible to maximize your success. Think of us as your coaches, helping you coach your family into the team we know it can be.

# 1

# CHANGE YOURSELF AND THEY WILL FOLLOW

Does this sound like you?

- "The kids don't help with a thing around here."
- "I can't get them to keep their rooms clean."
- "The hamper's loaded with laundry; the sink's loaded with dishes, and there are a dozen toys underfoot."
- "I work all day and then I have to come home and work all night or nothing would ever get done."
- "They say they'll help, but they don't do a thing unless I nag, nag, nag."
- "It's easier to do it myself than waste time arguing."

A lot of parents sound like this before they use the methods in this book, so you're in good company.

Like so many others, if you've solved the chore problems at your house by attempting to be Super Mom or Super Dad and doing it all, ask yourself why you do that. Most parents wear the "Super Parent" cape partly because they think it's their job, partly because it's not worth their effort to get uncooperative workers involved, and mainly because they don't know what else to do. But there are some serious consequences to this behavior. Aside from feeling exhausted and resentful, you're taking away many important opportunities for your children. You're also sending them into the world without the skills and ability to handle the logistics of life.

How could you possibly be depriving your children by doing everything for them? It's hard to imagine, but here's just some of what they miss out on: the ability to perform even the simplest everyday life tasks, the opportunity to be team players, the expectation to treat others respectfully, the pride that comes with making a difference and contributing to the family, the practice at being responsible and managing time, the strengthening of a "work hard" muscle, and the development of true self-worth and self-confidence. We know these are qualities you want your children to have. We also know that you may not realize you have one of the best opportunities for teaching these skills right at your fingertips—good old-fashioned "chores."

We'd like to help you make some changes around your household, because we know that it will be well worth your effort. We'll do our part to make involving the family in chores practical, fun, and easy. But we need some help from you. Here's what's required: *since you're in charge, you need to change yourself first.* That invites others to follow. We want you to focus on four elements: give up blame, change your behavior, change how you think, and create new mental pictures. That's easier said than done, and really, why should you have to do that work, too? Because it is what is needed for success.

## GIVE UP BLAME

"But isn't it really their fault?" you ask. Why should you have to change? Looking for blame won't solve your problems, but sometimes it makes you feel better, right? In addition to blaming your family members, you could also blame genetics. Surely you can prove your kids are as lazy as Great Aunt Tillie or Uncle George-on-her-side-of-the-family. You could blame the trauma from the divorce to explain your kids' lack of follow-through and procrastination. That would explain why you're not getting anywhere. How about blaming astrology? Maybe it's a sign thing. Can a Capricorn do toilets? Aren't Cancers the ones who love their homes and housework? Blaming it on your parents is still in vogue. Aren't they at fault because they didn't teach you how to work as a team player?

While we're on the subject of looking for blame, how about blaming science for failing to develop a pill or cure for the forgetfulness your children seem to have when it comes to keeping their agreements, or for the lack of focus when it comes to doing household tasks? There's usually a quick fix for everything today, so why isn't there a way to find one for doing chores? There's fast food, flash-frozen meals, e-mail, fax machines, instant everything. Where's the instant fix for uncooperative family members? To date, none has been found, but don't let that stop you from hoping and looking.

You could even blame history, if you need a culprit to make you feel better. When people lived on farms, everyone needed to help to survive. During World War II, when the men went to war and women took over their jobs to keep the country running, children's efforts were needed and valued at home. After the war, when the men came back, they needed their jobs, so women had to find something else to do. Seemed like being a "housewife" became the important job for women. Right about that time, Madison Avenue advertisers attempted to convince women that spending hours putting that special shine on the kitchen floor and the dining room furniture while popping homemade cookies in the oven was the road to fulfillment and joy. Obviously, marketing professionals both succeeded and failed simultaneously. Women baked a lot of cookies, but for the most part, many ended up feeling depressed, resentful, and angry. Men didn't fare much better, because having to live by strictly defined roles led them to feel trapped and claustrophobic. This eventually led to a lot of divorces, a lot of stepparent situations, and a lot of single parents. The family just isn't what it used to be, so how can you get folks working together?

If all this blame isn't enough, you could blame the trend to have more, more, and more. It must be greed's fault. To meet these demands for more, it takes two working parents. Who has time to teach the kids how to help the family?

Unfortunately, thinking up people or situations to blame doesn't get the piles of dirty dishes spread out on the coffee table cleaned up, or stop family members from accusing you of being a nag. *Looking for blame only puts off finding solutions to the problem.* While you agonize over how you got here, your kids are missing out on learning to contribute and you're missing out on living in a home that is peaceful and connected.

If your approach to taking the war out of chores has been to find blame, we know your efforts have been futile. What works better is to accept that you are the one in charge and that it's up to you to change yourself *first*. This by no means suggests that you are to blame. It's simply a practical first step that gets things moving in a different direction.

## CHANGE YOUR BEHAVIOR

Do this simple experiment to help you see just how powerful it is when you change what you do. Instead of nagging and yelling to motivate the other family members, grab a book or magazine, sit down on the couch, and start reading. Don't stop until someone notices you there. It probably won't take long before some family member asks, "Are you okay? What are you doing? Do you feel sick? Is something wrong? Who's making dinner?" Coincidentally, this will probably be the same family member who has been most deaf to your requests/demands for help. Notice that when you make even the smallest behavioral change, someone in your family takes notice. It's your first step.

This book is filled with suggestions to help you change yourself by changing what you do. As you read the book, highlight suggestions for changing your behavior and refer back to them often. When you feel like you're losing ground or relapsing into old patterns, start by looking at your behavior instead of wasting your time trying to figure out what others are doing. Then reread your highlighted suggestions and try again to change what you do.

## CHANGE HOW YOU THINK

You may end up pleasantly surprised at how much you can change by simply adjusting your attitude. There's a big difference between your attitude and your behavior. Your attitude is made up of the thoughts that you are aware of and the beliefs that are just below the surface and hidden from you. Your attitude influences the degree of success you'll experience.

Since part of your attitude is hidden from you, here's a simple way to get in touch with it. To find out what you really believe about chores or family work, pretend you are making a sign to hang in your kitchen that expresses your thoughts about chores. If that is too difficult, imagine what sign might have been hanging in the kitchen of the house you grew up in. Here are some examples:

- Chores are a good way to have fun.
- Anything you say, honey.
- Chores—yuck!

- Chores are mundane and unimportant.
- I don't mind doing chores if you'd just remind me.
- Work before play.
- Chores are tedious and I don't do routines.
- Chores are the necessities of life.

What would your sign say? Whatever it says, it speaks volumes to your current belief about chores. These hidden beliefs tend to run your life.

Let's look at some of these beliefs about chores and how they might affect cooperation at home. Here's one: "Children are only young once and they deserve to have a childhood that is fun and easy." Would this parent be expecting the kids to join in the family work? Probably not. Here's another: "It's my job to do the work around the house because I'm the adult, the woman, the man, the responsible one (you fill in the blank)." If you think that way and someone in the family complains because you're not doing your job, you'd probably give in and do everything yourself. How far would you get with the attitude that says, "Kids better do as I say, because I'm the boss"? No one really likes to be ordered about. Demands rarely invite participation and cooperation.

It may be time for you to start adjusting your attitude to invite cooperation. If you grew up with traditional values and still believe that there are separate and definite roles for men, women, and children to fulfill, you could adjust your attitude by reminding yourself that chores are just jobs that need to be done and they don't come with pink or blue ribbons.

If you believe that men are the breadwinners and women are the homemakers, step back and remind yourself that what you do is a choice, not an inherited trait.

If you were expected to do as you were told when growing up, you probably expect your children to do as they are told now, and wonder why they don't. Adjust your attitude and tell yourself that even though it may seem strange to sit down with your children and make decisions about household responsibilities together, it is another option. If your parents told you to go out and play and not to worry about work until you got older, you may have decided work is a burden and helping the family is a drudge or someone else's job. Rather than sending that message to your children, adjust your attitude and repeat to yourself, "When everyone helps, the load is lighter."

If your family divided chores by sex, age, or some other arbitrary method when you were growing up, you may find it difficult to let go of the old assumption of how it "should be done."

Many women feel guilty asking for help or not doing all the work inside the home like their mothers used to. In spite of their resentment, they feel uncomfortable stepping out of a traditional role of being in charge of home and hearth. They have no model or picture that shows them how to include their partner or children without feeling guilty, without thinking they are doing something wrong. At the same time, women are often afraid to give up the power that comes with managing their homes. They are also reluctant to involve their spouses and children, as they haven't yet learned how to include others in day-to-day decision making and household management. If any of these are your thoughts, adjust your attitude by reminding yourself that you are working at finding healthier new ways to think and act to replace those outdated and disrespectful beliefs.

Men often believe that working outside the home to earn a living is a sufficient contribution to the family. Unfortunately, many men continue to believe this even when their wives also work outside the home. Even when both parents work outside the home, the old values are hard to shake, often leaving one family member struggling to keep up with the endless tasks necessary to maintain the household. Adjust your attitude by telling yourself that give-and-take makes for happier, healthier, longer-lasting relationships.

Can you really change your beliefs? Yes. You formed them, so you can change them. If you're hoping for a family that becomes more of a team, you'll be surprised what a difference it makes when you tell yourself that your family members *want* to help each other. People in the family will pick up your energy when you believe in give-and-take and expect them to do something nice for each other because it's supportive and the right thing to do.

## CREATE NEW MENTAL PICTURES

In the next chapter, we'll help you implement a mental picture of your family as a team with you as the coach. Everyone on your team may have a different job, but they are included on the team because work around the house is everybody's job. That includes dads, moms, grandparents, little kids, big kids, roommates, and anyone else who is part of your household. As is true for any team, success takes time, practice, reasonable expectations, coaching, more practice, and a winning spirit. It doesn't happen overnight, but it's worth the effort.

You'll be pleasantly surprised when you create a mental picture of your team taking small steps, focusing on one thing at a time, and practicing it until it becomes routine. Picture setting up a family work time. Imagine how much fun it could be to make all the beds in the house—together while listening to loud, wild music. Wouldn't a family treasure hunt for dirty glasses and dishes be a lark? Think what could be accomplished with just ten minutes of folding clothes or putting away laundry. You'll be surprised at how much you can do in ten minutes when everyone is helping. See yourself in the center of all this, encouraging, helping, teaching, and laughing.

## A FEW WORDS OF CAUTION

Some family members may be highly motivated to change while others resist change at any cost. Members who have participated the least often feel the most threatened by the change. These family members worry that the changes will place an extra burden on them and may think, "If I start helping with one thing, there may be no end to the demands to do more. Besides working full time, I'll have to do all the housework, too." Inexperienced workers may fear looking stupid because they believe they should know how to do the job already. Some may have a hard time fitting in the extra jobs while others may resist giving up some of their free time.

When family members who previously did most of the family work delegate, they may enjoy the help at first, but later worry that others won't do the jobs correctly. Sometimes they struggle with their identity, thinking they are worthwhile only when they are the helpful, responsible, capable member of the family (some of those hidden attitudes). At first, family members who once did most of the chores may feel lost and guilty relaxing. It's hard for those used to doing something all the time to put their feet up, read a book, go for a walk, talk to a friend, or take time to smell the flowers.

Children may see helping as a game at first, but later, as they realize helping is "a way of life," the jobs become a burden. If children have gotten used to parents providing "maid," "janitorial," or "restaurant" service, they miss this when it's gone. Many children welcome the chance to have more say, but view their new responsibilities as a loss of freedom.

You've got your work cut out for you, but we'll be with you every step of the way, helping with tips, suggestions, and encouragement. We've been down this road and know that it's worth the effort. It's easier to *do* than to *undo*, so the sooner you start taking the "chore" out of chores and building a family team, the easier it will be for all of you.

# 2

# THE SECRETS OF CREATING FAMILY TEAMWORK

Today is the first day of your life as the family coach. What are you up against? What does your team look like? How much work will it take to get them in shape? If you've been doing most of the work, think of your teammates as people who have been living with a full staff of servants (you, you, and you). You've cooked, cleaned, entertained, chauffeured, made sure backpacks are in order, homework done, appointments scheduled, and that's just the beginning. Most of your energy has been spent making life as pleasant as possible for everyone. Nice, right? For them, maybe, but not for you. And today, you're going to begin changing that.

Here's what you say: "I'd like some help." Here's what they hear: "I'd like you to do things you don't want to." Can you imagine your family members jumping up and down for joy saying, "Oh thank you, thank you for not doing everything for us anymore"? More likely they would be shocked, disbelieving, angry, scared, and determined to get you back in their service, or hire new servants.

If you've been "a full staff of servants" for your family members, this analogy may help you imagine their reaction to the changes they'll be experiencing. Though the tips in this chapter can make your job of winning family cooperation easier, household members will take time adjusting and getting on the same page as you. You, on the other hand, knowing that you've made up your mind to do it differently, want everything to change immediately. We understand. We empathize. But we are here to remind you that a new way of doing things is a concept that takes many steps to reach. To help you on your journey, we recommend following our six suggestions for winning cooperation.

## SIX STEPS TO WINNING FAMILY COOPERATION

You're the one who is going to change first, remember? So here's how to go about it to minimize the chaos and aggravation that can result from changing your role in the family. Memorize this short list, and say it over and over to yourself throughout the day. You can even sing it to yourself to the tune of "Are You Sleeping? (Brother John)." If you can't remember what you're doing, no one else will either.

> We're a team,
> I'm the coach,
> Step back, slow down. Step back, slow down.
> Focus your attention,
> Have a conversation,
> Follow through, follow through.

These simple six lines contain all the basics, but here's what the steps look like in a little more detail.

1. *Think of your family as a team.* Everyone living in the house is part of the problem and needs to be part of the solution. First, instead of trying to get chores done, your job is to build the team by strengthening family relationships, involving others, sharing the load, dividing work by ability and age, holding everyone accountable, and creating opportunities to build self-esteem. A team works best when everyone is on the same side.

2. *You have a new role and it is "team coach."* To be a good coach, you'll need to understand the game, have a strategy, know how to build teamwork, motivate and encourage others, and build fun into the game. Your job is also to build skills while inspiring others to treat each other well and conduct themselves respectfully. This is no small task and it doesn't have to happen overnight. You have a lifetime with your family, and the effort you put in at the beginning pays off exponentially down the road.

3. *Slow down; take a step back.* You've been reacting and operating like a trained seal—trained by your family members who are invested in keeping you doing the work while they don't. Now is the time to sit back and notice what is going on. Think of those coaches who spend hours watching and rewatching game films. While they're in the middle of the game, they can't see everything. But when they take a step back and slow things down, they can target the areas that need work. That's what you need to do. As you see the problems, you can decide what you will or won't do, knowing that doing more of the same won't work. It's time to come up with a new plan.

4. *Focus your attention by deciding on the first three small steps you'll take.* Don't make the plan elaborate. The simpler the plan, the better the chance of it working. When you get too complex, no one, including you, can remember what you decided or what you were working on. You're the coach, so you need to inform your teammates about what is going to happen and let them know that once things are underway and you've tried out

the new system, you'd love to have their input about any changes or tweaking that is needed. This step is the one that seems to require the most coaching from you, so be sure to check the examples in this chapter to help you succeed.

5. *Begin a conversation/dialogue instead of immediately solving the problem.* Previously you gave orders or left lists or nagged or made ultimatums. Now, you're inviting a dialogue. You do this by starting with your idea, communicating it to the others in simple language with as few words as possible, and letting them know that their input is important. This shifts your relationship with family members from boss to coach, which is a recipe for success. Here's how it might sound: "I've figured out a way we could help each other at dinnertime. I'll cook and you guys can take turns cleaning up and setting the table. We'll start tonight. If we don't like how this works, we can talk about it at dinner or on Sunday to see if we can figure out another way to do things." You're the leader and at the same time you've created an invitation for conversation and built in a time to talk together.

6. *Follow through by doing what you said you would do.* Before you decided to make changes, you probably tried to get others to do what you wanted. That worked about as well as trying to swim up a waterfall. That is because you can't make anyone else do anything. Now all you have to do is what you said you were going to do, which is much easier. Using the example from #5, all the coach has to do is cook dinner and let the rest happen as it happens. If he or she can maintain a sense of humor and curiosity, it's entirely possible that within a day or two, the rest of the family will figure out how to fill in the pieces that need to be done. If not, there's always time for conversation.

Implementing the six steps can create success. Here's how it looked for Grandma Lynnie (one of the authors), when her sixteen-month-old grandson, Zachary, discovered the spigot for the water cooler and made it his favorite toy, creating a large puddle of water on the floor. Her first response was to turn the cooler around so Zachary couldn't see the spigot. That worked for about five minutes. Her second response was to say, "No," but she didn't feel good about having to hover and bark orders while her grandbaby played with the spigot.

When she took some time to think about the situation after Zachary went home, she realized that this would be an opportunity to introduce the concept of teamwork (step #1) to her grandson. She thought of herself as a coach whose job it was to teach Zachary when and how to use the cooler to help the family (step #2). She was able to think clearly because she wasn't in the middle of the mess (step #3). She decided that the next time Zachary came to visit she'd meet him at the door with a bowl, lead him to the cooler, and hold the bowl under the spigot for as long as he felt like running the water (step #4).

The next time Zachary came to visit, he headed to the cooler right on schedule, and Grandma Lynnie met him with the dog dish. While he filled the dish, she said, "Thanks for helping Grandma fill the water bowl for the dog. I like it when you help me. You can use the water cooler when Grandma is with you and she has something that needs filling." Zachary bobbed his head up and down in agreement (step #5). Everytime Zachary headed toward the cooler, Grandma Lynnie grabbed a vessel to fill and stood by while he worked the spigot. She thanked him profusely for helping Grandma (step #6).

The following week, the two repeated the process, but by week three, Zachary was on to new territory, the water cooler seemingly forgotten. But when Grandma needed to fill a coffee cup or glass, all she had to do was call for his help, and the little guy was ready to work the spigot and do his first "chore" at Grandma's house.

You may be thinking that it's easy for a grandmother who only sees her grandson once a week to take the time for training herself and her grandson, and of course, you would be right. It's much harder to have the patience for teaching the family when you're running as fast as you can to get things done or keep everything under control. The notion that things are under control is a fallacy, because in reality, nothing is in control. You are simply managing chaos. It doesn't feel good, but it's the demon you know, like Sally, in the following story.

## IMPATIENCE AND UNREALISTIC EXPECTATIONS CAN SPOIL THE BEST OF INTENTIONS

Sally was a parent with unrealistic expectations and a lot of resentment. She insisted her family meet with her counselor to get them to help out at home. The counselor helped the family with the six steps, and everyone reluctantly agreed to do two chores each day for a week. They agreed to reevaluate at the next session.

The day after the counseling session, Sally came home from work expecting to see the chores done but walked into a disaster area instead. In a rage, she stood in front of the TV set and yelled.

"Look at this mess. I've been at work all day and I come home to toys, shoes, and magazines all over the living room floor. When you were at the counselor's, you agreed to pick up each day. There are dirty dishes in the living room and piles of clean laundry on the sofa. I suppose you're waiting for me to fold everything. You told the counselor you would help, and now you aren't keeping your promises. Gary, is that your dirty laundry? What have you been doing all day? No one cares about me!"

Sally's goal is to get her family members to be more respectful, but her methods don't invite cooperation. If she wants to live in a family where people ask, "What can I do to help?" she needs to reevaluate her attitude about perfection and justice. She also needs to work on more reasonable expectations and smaller steps.

If Sally reminded herself that the family is a team and she is the coach, she could step back and slow down. From the comfort of the couch, with her feet up and a cup of tea in her hand, she might decide that everyone could work together for ten to fifteen minutes when she got home, and the chores would get done without a battle. Sally could take time to say hello to everyone and then inform them that when she got home, before starting dinner, she'd appreciate if everyone would do the two chores at the same time. If that didn't work, she'd be happy to entertain other suggestions, but first, it would be great to try out her idea. Imagine the response she'd get from her family members if she stopped biting their heads off!

## DOES CHANGE HAVE TO BE SO SLOW?

You might be thinking Sally is moving at a turtle's pace, which is true. She is, but it's a step in a new direction. It is important to create a success to build on. Spending ten minutes a day for a week or two getting everyone used to helping and being a teammate goes a long way to alleviating a lot of the problems. Doing more of what doesn't work won't build teamwork. There are signs all around you that say when you're pushing too hard and your team members aren't on the same side. Look for them and if you spot them, slow down and go back to the six steps for winning family cooperation.

Here are seven signs of a lack of cooperation you need to be on guard for:

1. *Unresolved grievances.* It is unlikely that people who share a household have the same daily living habits. Some people like the TV or radio on for background noise and others can't stand anything but complete silence. Some people squeeze the toothpaste in the middle; others squeeze the tube at the end. Rarely do two people have the same standards for cleanliness. But when such gripes become sources of constant irritation without hope of resolution, this unwillingness to work together can tear households apart.

2. *Constant complaints.* "That's not fair! I have to do everything around here." "You never keep your promises." "Stop acting

like my mother." "That's a man's (woman's) job, so I'm not going to do it." Do any of these complaints sound familiar? They are signs of building resentment. If unheeded, they soon escalate and erode relationships.

3. *Imbalance in work distribution.* One person often decides that it's less hassle to do what needs to be done than to argue, nag, or put up with the chaos. A feeling of hopelessness often leads to the decision to do more than a fair share. Taking on too much demonstrates both lack of self-respect and lack of respect for others. Family members lose out on opportunities to contribute and build skills when everything is done for them. One person's overdoing is also a sign that other family members are willing to take advantage, consciously or unconsciously, of the household member who has the lowest tolerance for certain forms of chaos and this breeds resentment and discontent.

4. *Arbitrary assignment of responsibilities* (by age, sex, or other categories). Operating by assumptions instead of agreements creates no-win situations in a household. Just because someone's mother cleaned the windows and attended to the inside of the house while the father organized the garage and took care of the outside chores doesn't mean there are no alternatives. If someone insists that his or her way is the only way or the right way, that person is being arbitrary and closed-minded instead of cooperative.

5. *Conflict avoidance.* Every household has things family members disagree about. Thinking problems will go away by themselves is a delusion. The result of this "magical thinking" is putting up with feelings of irritation, aggravation, and anger instead of practicing problem solving and resolving issues. Avoiding conflict by saying nothing leads to more serious friction in the family. Since family members aren't mind readers, they can't work together to solve problems unless they know what the problems are.

6. *Yelling, threatening, nagging, bribing, coercing, demanding.* These behaviors inhibit cooperation and if they are the primary tools for gaining assistance, they will result in rebellion or passive resistance. Family members may say yes with their words but no with their actions by not following through. A rash of forgetfulness or an abundance of promises to do a job later may mean that someone in the family is using motivational methods that invite undesirable behaviors instead of enlisting cooperation.

7. *Blaming and fault finding.* Looking for blame and finding fault are sidetracks to real problem solving. Family members feel hurt and picked on when others attack them instead of attacking the problem.

If you recognize any of these seven signs in your family, you know it will be worth your effort to keep singing our song till it becomes a way of life. Ready now? One and two and three and four:

We're a team,
I'm the coach,
Step back, slow down. Step back, slow down.
Focus your attention,
Have a conversation,
Follow through, follow through.

# 3

# GOOD COACHES BUILD
# WINNING TEAMS

Consider this chapter your coaching clinic. We wish we could fly you to a resort where you could relax while learning, but alas, we know you barely have time to read the chapter. So we'll make it as painless as possible.

Let's start with what kind of coach you are right now. What are your strengths? What are your shortcomings? What are your methods for motivation? If you're not sure, here's a way to figure that out. If you had a tape recorder or video camera filming you while you were trying to get help around the house, what would you sound like? Look like? Would you be Bossy Bart, barking orders and making threats? Would you be Rachael the Rug, begging, pleading, and offering bribes? Would you be Millie the Mouse, asking so softly that no one listens? Would you be Norton Neglectful, showing up and hoping for help? How about Critical Carla, pointing out everyone's mistakes? Just for fun, give yourself a name that represents your current coaching style.

If you believe your style could use some improvement, remember back to someone who inspired you to learn. Was it a teacher, a relative, a camp counselor, a friend, a parent, a minister, a coach, a teammate? What was it they did that impressed and motivated you? What would happen if you were to pattern yourself after them?

Betsy loved her basketball coach and said she would do anything for him. "Yeah, he was a screamer, but he was fair, fair, fair. And he motivated us and taught us how to be a team. He treated everyone equally—no favorites, and he always did what he said he'd do. If we missed a practice, we didn't get to play in the game, no matter how good our excuse was or how good a player we were or how far behind the team was. You can imagine what great attendance he had at practices after the first time one of us had to sit out a game on the bench. He didn't humiliate us, either. When he told us to sit on the bench, he'd say, 'You missed practice so you'll have to sit on the bench. It's only one game. You'll be fine.' And we were. We trusted him to help us be better people and better players." Betsy modeled her coaching style after him and named herself *Be Fair Betsy*.

Sam had a camp counselor who taught him how to paddle a canoe. The counselor was very strict, but very knowledgeable. Once Sam and the others learned the basic skills, the counselor took them on harder and harder courses so they could experience the power and exhilaration that came from improving their skills through practice. If Sam was looking for a nickname for his coaching style, it might be *Strict Sam*.

Frank's dad made everything fun. No matter what the chore, he had a way of turning it into a game. Frank modeled his leadership style after his dad, thinking of himself as *Fun Frank*. His kids never balked at helping. Frank also knew the value of treats after work. The Popsicle in the back yard or the ice cream cone went a long way to revive his tired crew. That came after the work was done and not as a carrot to entice them to do the work.

Earlene thought about one of her teachers whom she considered the best teacher she ever had. Why? Miss Brownley saw ability in everyone in her class and found special jobs for each of them. Earlene was in charge of decorating the bulletin boards. Her friend Sarah erased the board, while her classmate Craig blew the whistle when it was time to come in from recess. Miss Brownley never raised her voice and always had a ready smile when the class assembled each day. When asked what her coaching nickname would be, Earlene said, "Why, Encouraging Earlene, of course."

As you can see, there isn't one style for everyone, but the winning coaches were all encouraging and empowering. They adopted five coaching strategies that you can do, too: *value differences, invite participation, use the language of encouragement, hold young people accountable,* and *teach skills.*

---

## COACHING STRATEGY #1: VALUE DIFFERENCES

Valuing differences creates openness, curiosity, and the desire to help. Ask your teammates for their ideas. Stand back and see what they do before you jump in with suggestions. Consider living with a new way to do things for a while to see if it ends up being a better way.

---

Getting caught up in thinking yours is the right way can be very discouraging. There is no "right way"—only *your* right way—because it's based on your subjective thinking. There are always many ways to think. Have you noticed how children resist cleaning their rooms? You may have created this "monster" by insisting they use your "right" way to clean their bedroom. When you focus on progress instead of your picture of perfection, you get better results.

Sheryl decided to shift her attitude, and found she enjoyed her four-year-old daughter's idea of a clean bedroom. The bed was made (but the bedspread was full of lumps) and the floor was clean (the toys were all are pushed under the bed), and Martine showed off her work with great pride.

Sheryl snapped her picture and put it up for all to see. Whenever a visitor came, Martine led them to the picture and told them that she was cleaning her own room now.

If your children cleaned the room themselves and are proud of their work, focus on their enthusiasm and sense of accomplishment. Like Sheryl, you may even learn to love a lumpy bed!

If you persist in setting the standards, you could be inviting problems. Your idea of "clean," "organized," or "straightened" may not be the same as another's. Honoring another person's way of thinking, a rather challenging concept, can lead to creative new ideas and a sense of "our household," like in Joanie's case.

When Joanie's boyfriend moved out and she needed help with the rent, she asked her friend Pam to move in. Pam had two young children and was excited to move from her apartment to a house. Joanie was careful to point out where things went and how she liked things. As a result, Pam had a hard time feeling like this was home.

Joanie came home one day to find that Pam had reorganized "her" kitchen. At first she was angry because the changes made it hard for her to function, but she soon realized that this drastic measure accomplished two important things: first, her new roommate's children were able to reach and find things more easily; and second, the ownership of the kitchen had changed from "Joanie's" to "the family's."

Pam also introduced some new cleaning products that worked better than Joanie's old ones. Her children wanted to try out the new product one of their friends' mothers used. They had such a good time making the bathtub sparkle after their bath that they asked if they could clean the tub and sink on cleaning day. Joanie realized that by making room for new ideas she was encouraging involvement.

In another family, Chris helped his wife consider a new strategy when he got involved in the grocery shopping. Mom and the kids had always divided the list at the store, even though it was difficult and bothersome. When Chris started shopping with the family, he suggested dividing the list at home, where everyone could sit at the table and write down their items. This worked much better, and in no time, list making became a game, with everyone shouting out the items he or she wanted to find at the store. Instead of insisting there was only one way to do things, Chris's wife realized the benefits of changing her thinking.

*Coaching Tip #1*: Replace, "My way or the highway" with "*What are your suggestions for doing this job?*" It's a starting point that focuses on progress, not perfection, and invites family members to want to be on the team.

## COACHING STRATEGY #2: INVITE PARTICIPATION

Your attitude isn't the only thing that gets in the way of being encouraging. Your actions can make or break your team members' participation. If you are constantly redoing others' work or correcting them while they work, it won't take long before they decide to stop helping. Your actions speak louder than your words. If you say you want help, but redo everything family members do, they can see you don't really mean what you say.

You have a decision to make. What is more important: having a "perfect" house or encouraging family members to participate? If you wish to be more encouraging, these actions are the ones you'll want to use: do nothing and bite your tongue; teach on the fly; make it a game; work together; and celebrate. Here's how they look:

Jack decided that a great way to involve his kids in family work was to let them help take care of the plants. He picked that as a starting point because his kids loved to play with water and liked to hang out with him in the garden. He put his three-year-old in charge of watering the outside plants and his four-year-old in charge of watering the inside ones.

He showed both kids how to do the job and then handed over the hose and the watering can. His three-year-old gave each outside plant a splash of water. His four-year-old gave each inside plant enough water to drown the plant, along with an extra spray on the furniture. Jack bit his tongue. Instead of correcting the kids, he thanked them for helping him out. When they went off to play, he wiped the extra water off the furniture and gave the outside plants more water.

Was Jack teaching his kids to be irresponsible? Shouldn't he expect them to learn to do the job correctly? We think that Jack was making an excellent decision by first focusing on involvement instead of perfection. He'll have plenty of time to add to the training. Next time his four-year-old waters the house plants, he might say, "Hey, Buddy, let's throw a towel over your shoulder so if there are drips on the furniture, you can wipe them off." There's always time to learn more, but first, you want your kids to feel good about helping.

You can teach as you go instead of making the initial training time an ordeal. We call this "teaching on the fly." If you're cooking and your child says, "Can I help?" say "Yes!" and demonstrate how to crack an egg or stir the soup. When your roommate walks into the kitchen and asks what you're doing, show him how to use the pasta machine. When your wife says, "I can't pound a nail in straight," hand her the hammer and say, "Go for it. Bent nails are easy to replace."

You'll notice that in our examples, the focus is on work and chores as a fun time together, not a drag. By emphasizing the fun of work and making it a game whenever possible, you'll get more help. Have a race putting things away, or set the timer and try to "beat the clock." Clean up papers by taking turns "shooting" them into the wastebasket. Pitch things into the toy box from a few feet away. Write chores on pieces of paper and pick them out of a bag. Wear bathing suits to wash the cars and spray each other. Make an assembly line to pass dirty dishes to the sink.

You may also have noticed that in most of the situations we describe, family members are working together. Schedule a "work time" when everyone is doing a job at the same time, even if each job is different. Try this when preparing dinner, doing yard work, cleaning up before bedtime, and preparing for holidays. Why? Because work gets done and gets done faster when everyone is doing it together. You've probably seen how ineffective it is for many (if not most) kids when you leave them a list. (If you have family members who work well from a list, go for it. We wouldn't want to discourage you from using what works.) We know that not all work will be fun but we believe that as a coach with a little creative thinking, you have many opportunities to turn work into fun.

A family of three decided to set aside a day for home improvements every six months. Between work days they kept a list of projects needing attention. A few days before the chosen work day, one of the parents took the list to the hardware store and purchased all the supplies that would be needed to succeed in completing the tasks. On the work day, the family members tackled the list together and were amazed at how quickly the work got done. They finished so easily that they decided to do a few chores that weren't on the list and then go out and celebrate with a pizza.

You can see what a natural progression it is to want to celebrate when work becomes fun and chores get done. There are many ways you can do this. Take instant pictures of family members standing next to a finished job. Use your digital camera and start a photo scrapbook in the computer that all can access. Display the pictures on the refrigerator or bulletin board. Have a barbecue or play a game when the household work is finished. Take yourselves to a movie or out to dinner. Make a special dessert.

---

*Coaching Tip #2*: By *replacing your critical face with a smile* and making chores fun, you'll go a long way toward encouraging others to work with you.

---

---

## COACHING STRATEGY #3:
## USE ENCOURAGING WORDS

Be aware that how you say things affects the direction you'll head. Your words may invite a result opposite from what you intend. If you think you're being encouraging, but household members resist your efforts, check your language. In trying to motivate, you may actually be discouraging them.

---

How does this happen? To gain insight, look at the examples below to see if you inadvertently send the wrong message.

| If You Say This: | Others Might Hear: |
| --- | --- |
| Let me do it! | You're not capable. |
| Go out and play. | Parents work, kids play. |
| You're too little. | You're not competent. |
| That's not the way. | You don't do things right. |
| Here, I can do that. | You're not capable of learning. |
| I don't do it this way. | You did it wrong. |
| You never do anything to help! | You're a bad person. |

To develop an encouraging way of speaking, think about what you want to communicate. When you show respect and appreciation and focus on the efforts and improvements others make, you have a much better chance of sounding encouraging. Be glad that others are involved and let them know how much their help is appreciated. Then build on the successes you have. The following messages convey encouragement, promote cooperation, and instill confidence.

| If You Say This: | Others Might Hear: |
| --- | --- |
| Let's do this together so it goes faster. | We can help each other. |
| You try. | You're able to do things. |
| Here's the DustBuster so you can help! | Work can be enjoyable. |
| You can do it. | You're capable. |
| Thank you. That really helped. | Your help is appreciated. |
| What would happen if you add half a cup? | You're able to figure things out. |
| Cleanup time. Let's work together. | Everyone can contribute. |

Words of encouragement focus on gratitude, appreciation, acceptance, effort, and uniqueness. At first, it takes effort to think of encouraging things to say, but the results make the effort worthwhile. Thinking, acting, and speaking positively also apply to fostering responsibility. You can prevent irresponsibility by having a positive, optimistic outlook. Telling yourself "they will" instead of "they won't" can create a positive outcome. Still, no matter how positive your attitude, agreements will be broken or forgotten at times. You can foster responsibility by trusting that mistakes are opportunities to learn and remembering the most encouraging words of all, "Try again."

---

*Coaching Tip #3*: Make sure your language matches your new coaching style. *Replace criticism and judgments with positive thoughts and words.*

---

## COACHING STRATEGY #4:
## HOLD OTHERS ACCOUNTABLE

If a family member forgets a job, often a simple question like "What happened? I noticed the garbage is overflowing in the kitchen" can get things back on track. Jobs not completed on a regular basis indicate that you have a responsibility problem that needs attention. If the original plan was reasonable and realistic and you feel frustrated because the work is being done poorly or not done at all, it may be time to set up either natural consequences or active follow-through.

---

Natural consequences allow people to find out what would happen if you did nothing. For instance, if one of your children "forgets" to set the table, you might call the family to dinner and say nothing. The "forgetful" child would quickly remember he or she agreed to set the table.

If your roommate forgets she agreed to cook, you could read a book or watch TV as if nothing were wrong. As it gets later, someone would get hungry and wonder about dinner. The key is to do and say nothing and allow the "forgetful" helper to experience the consequences of his or her behavior. Natural consequences are most effective with older kids and adults who might use chores as a battleground for fighting with you.

Sometimes using active follow-through makes more sense than waiting to see what will happen if you do nothing. It is often confusing to parents as to how to go about this. When a family member has agreed to do something and then "forgotten," most parents don't feel respected and don't want to act respectfully. They wonder why they should have to suffer when it's their child who didn't keep an agreement.

This is why you are at a coaching clinic. It's time for you to learn some new strategies. Remember, you're building a team consisting of family members who get stronger and stronger at being responsible and respectful. It'll be worth your effort, even though in the beginning it takes some time. Here's an example of what active follow-through might look like if someone agrees to mow the lawn but "forgets."

In this situation it would be impractical to use a natural consequence and do nothing because you don't want to watch the lawn turn to hay (nor do your neighbors). If you are concerned about the yard, active follow-through might be more useful. When you set up the chore, say to the one responsible for mowing, "Not cutting the lawn when you've agreed to is not a choice. Since I'm unwilling to nag and remind, we need to decide on something that will help you remember to cut the lawn as agreed. It must be related, reasonable, and respectful. Do you have any ideas? Let's brainstorm."

Usually at this point, your children have no ideas, and probably, you don't either. You may have been used to nagging or punishing, lecturing or scolding, so your repertoire is severely limited. It's hard to think of an action you could take that would be logical, firm, kind, and get the job done. That's why we're going to help you with this one. Here are some options for the uncut lawn:

We suggest sitting down with your child and offering any of the following choices. You could agree that the lawn must be cut before dinner and that dinner waits until the lawn is cut. Another choice would be to agree that work comes before play and that TV, video games, computers, e-mails, phone calls, and friends have to wait until the lawn is mowed. You could also agree on setting up an inconvenient reminder in advance with your child. It sounds like this. "We could make a deal that you'll cut the lawn before a certain deadline. If you 'forget,' then you agree to be inconvenienced and do it during a favorite TV show." Another possibility would be to hire someone else to cut the lawn with the pay coming out of your child's funds.

If your child doesn't like any of the choices and can't come up with a different one, you pick which choice you'll try out for one week. Then agree on a deadline for the job to be done, because you can't follow through until someone misses the deadline (you sit and do nothing until it's past the deadline).

If you've been paying attention, by now you've realized that this process is going to be work for you. First you need to have the discussion, then you need to get agreement, then the two of you have to agree on a deadline, and finally, at the time of the deadline, you're the one who does the active follow-through. Here's how that would look: Your child agreed to have the lawn done before playing with friends. The friends arrive, and the lawn isn't done. You haven't said a word up to this point. You haven't reminded, coaxed, nagged, or hinted. Your son is ready to leave the house. You motion for your son to come to where you are seated and quietly, so as not to humiliate him in front of his friends, say, "What was our agreement? Have you kept it? Please do. Let your friends know they can wait in your room until you're done mowing the lawn." Your son, because he was part of the agreement, does as he promised without a fight . . . really!

You'll notice that the key word is *agree, agree, agree*. The actions that you will follow through on will only work if you and your child both agree in advance. Usually an agreement is made for a week or a month with the understanding that it can be changed after a certain time period when more information is available. Active follow-through means you have a conversation with your child, you make a deal, and then *you* follow through when they *don't*!

Here is another example of active follow-through one family used: Steve couldn't understand why his wife had been unable to get their twelve-year-old son, Rory, to clean his room. His fourteen-year-old daughter, Amy, always put everything in its place, but Rory was impossible, littering his floor with clothes and toys. His wife, Elaine, complained that she couldn't walk in Rory's room to get the laundry. She yelled and threatened, but the situation didn't improve.

After several weeks of attending a parenting class, Elaine was ready to tackle the problem in a new way. She talked with her husband and they agreed to meet with the children to discuss the problem. After Steve and Elaine shared their views on the problem, Amy piped in, "But I always clean my room."

Elaine said, "Amy, we aren't looking for blame, just solutions. We need to come up with a plan we can all live with." Everyone shared ideas and both kids agreed to clean their rooms once a week. They all decided that if their room wasn't done before Sunday morning, they could not go anywhere or do anything until it was done.

The following Sunday morning Rory's friends came by to ask him to go bike riding. When he asked his parents if he could go, they said, "Remember our agreement?" He told his friends he couldn't ride because he had work to do first. He was grumpy and sullen all day, but he did what he'd agreed to do. His parents knew the arrangement itself was lesson enough so they refrained from saying things like "Maybe next time you'll plan ahead!" or "Stop acting so grumpy; it's your own fault." It's important to understand that it's okay for children to have their feelings; if they're grumpy, give them a little space for their feelings while still holding them accountable for their behavior.

You may find that in spite of your best efforts, family members don't follow through. In such cases you can decide to work with family members to *make a deal*, or you can decide what you will (or will not) do in a situation and let the family know your decision in advance. Here, the important words are *in advance*. The idea is to hold family members accountable, not to punish them or insist that they suffer to learn.

Margie lived with her seven-year-old son, Lance. He agreed to pick up his toys each day. After a few weeks, Margie caught herself reminding Lance daily to pick up his toys. She told him that their plan wasn't working. Lance said, "I'll remember from now on. I'll pick up my toys."

Margie responded, "That's great. I'm glad to hear that, but I want to tell you what I've decided to do if you don't keep your agreement." Lance looked at her and asked, "What do you mean?"

In a friendly tone Margie said, "I'm not going to remind you or nag you anymore. I expect that you'll do what you say. If you haven't picked up your toys by 5:30 each evening, I'll figure you want me to do it. If I do it, I'll put the toys in a box called the 'Sunday Box,' and you can get them out the following Sunday."

The next few evenings Margie put a number of Lance's toys in the box. He started to scramble when he saw her putting his toys in the box. "I'm getting them," he shouted and raced around to pick them up. Margie noticed the floor was clear the next couple of nights and Lance was happy to get his toys back on Sunday. Although Lance left an occasional toy out after that, he usually had his toys picked up by 5:30 every day. If not, Margie simply followed through without words and put them in the "Sunday Box."

By letting family members know what the problem is and asking for their help in solving it, you sometimes discover that your expectations have been unrealistic or poorly thought out. For example, your teenage son may have agreed to take the garbage out on Tuesday nights but now has football practice that night. He gets home late and doesn't have time to do the job. He'd be willing to take the garbage out on Monday nights if you're willing to make the change.

If he still forgets, you might decide you are unwilling to make breakfast or to cook the next meal until the garbage is removed. Perhaps (with your son's agreement) you could seal the garbage bag and place it by the door to help him remember it's time to empty the garbage.

It takes time and creativity to find ideas that encourage rather than punish, but the result is cooperation and personal responsibility instead of intimidation or rebellion. You probably have been wasting a lot more time in the long run by nagging or doing for than it would take to sit down with your family members and brainstorm something creative or to do the active follow-through needed to hold someone accountable. In the spirit of fun, it's all worth a try, at least for a day, if not a week.

*Coaching Tip #4:* When they don't do what they agreed to do, it's your turn to go into motion. Hold others accountable by following through with the agreement you made, regardless of the attitude or behavior of the irresponsible family member. Remain kind and cool and calm, saying, "What was our deal? Are you planning to keep your agreement?" If not, then *do what you said you would do, quickly and without rancor.*

## COACHING STRATEGY #5: TEACH SKILLS

Frank asked Jack to remove the grass and dig out the earth so that they could build a patio. Jack was a hard worker, and he took the job very seriously. He removed all the grass and then started digging with a rounded shovel, painstakingly moving the dirt at a snail's pace. Frank came by and realized that he hadn't taken any time to show Jack how to do the job. He had assumed that everyone knew what he knew, forgetting that there had been a time when he was also a learner and someone showed him how to get work done.

Frank said to Jack, "Let me show you a little trick that might make the job go easier. Instead of starting with the shovel, use the mattock to chop up the dirt. Then use the rake to move the dirt into a pile. Finally, if you use the flat shovel, you'll be able to get more dirt up each time."

Jack looked crestfallen, and Frank quickly said, "Jack, I'm really sorry I didn't think to show you the tricks I learned when I was starting out. I made some pretty big assumptions that resulted in this job being a lot harder than it needed to be. You're a really good worker, and I appreciate all you have done. My suggestions are meant to add skills, not criticize."

Frank left the area and Jack took up the mattock and started chopping. It only took a few minutes for him to realize that there was a better and easier way to do the job. Before long, he was clearing the area like a pro.

Teaching skills is an important part of building a team. Don't make assumptions about *anything*. Just because you know how to boil an egg, clean a toilet, iron a shirt, turn on the washer, or wash the dog doesn't mean that someone who has never done the job will know what to do. Start with time for training, and make it as enjoyable as possible.

Sometimes training can be as simple as you showing or explaining to someone what needs to be done, like Frank did with Jack. Other times, training needs to be broken down into steps, starting with you doing the job to demonstrate, while others watch. Next, you do the job with the person. When they feel more comfortable, you observe from nearby while they do the job. Finally, you make yourself available as needed while they work alone.

Making work a game can motivate an untrained, unskilled worker to get involved and make a contribution. Beck's thirteen-year-old stepson, Keith, was a frequent dinner guest at the house. Keith was a bright, capable person. However, when it came time to clean up, Beck noticed that his stepson consistently disappeared.

One day Beck decided to go looking for Keith and ask for his help. He found him in his room playing a video game. Keith tried to get out of helping, but after some prodding, Beck discovered the real problem: his stepson had never done a dish in his life and didn't know how. Too embarrassed to admit this at his age, he avoided helping instead.

Beck said, "Keith, old buddy, today is your lucky day. I just happen to be ready to show you a trick I learned when I was in the Revolutionary War. Come on and give me a hand, and I'll show you."

"Wasn't that war a long time ago?" Keith asked.

"That's true, I was very young at the time, and all they would let me do were dishes. Let me show you a few shortcuts I learned as I washed dishes for thousands of soldiers day after day." Keith looked on with interest, even though he was pretty sure his stepfather wasn't really that old.

By making a game out of teaching Keith how to do dishes, Beck was able to help him save face and learn at the same time. Beck showed Keith how to use cleanser and a scrubbing pad to clean the broiler pan. "We used to use sand and rawhide, but these work almost as well," he teased.

A half hour later, after intense scrubbing, Keith produced the shiniest broiler pan in the family's history. Everyone raved about the great job. The next time he stayed for dinner, he jumped in to help, saying to his startled mother, "Let me show you some tricks Beck taught me that he learned doing dishes for the soldiers during the Revolutionary War."

Next, Beck asked Keith if he would like to learn some tricks from the Spanish-American War.

"You were in that one, too?" Keith exclaimed. "I didn't even know you were a soldier."

"Well Keith, I have to admit I didn't do any fighting because they kept me so busy in the kitchen. It was in that war that I really learned how to cook. Want me to teach you?"

"Sure," said Keith enthusiastically.

"Let's start by making your lunch for school. Now you could do a simple peanut butter sandwich, but the troops used to like something with a little more pizzazz. My specialty was called 'The Dagwood of All Dagwoods Sandwich.' First you shave some lettuce real thin. Then you cut green peppers into perfect rounds. The troops always liked hot peppers and onions, but they might give you indigestion. What do you think?"

"I want to make my sandwich just like you do, Beck."

"Okay. Then pay close attention," Beck continued. "I learned to spread the mustard and mayo with a spatula because it went faster.

Then I heap the lettuce, onions, green peppers, and hot peppers on like so. Next, I throw on some slices of your favorite lunch meat. The troops used to love buffalo, but they don't carry it at the grocery store so we'll have to settle for turkey. Now comes my secret ingredient. I sprinkle just a little vinegar on. You've got to be careful not to use too much, or the bread gets soggy and the troops complain. Hey, these look good enough to eat. What do you say, shall we have a snack and make some new ones for your lunch?" Keith knew that Beck hadn't been in any of the wars he talked about. In fact, he suspected Beck learned how to make his sandwich by watching the kid who worked at the deli down the street. But he liked learning from Beck because he made everything fun.

> *Coaching Tip #5: Take time for training.* Use your unique coaching style to help others learn how to get a job done, regardless of how big or small the job may be.

## TAKE TIME FOR TRAINING YOURSELF

You've probably attended plenty of clinics or workshops or lectures where you walked out thinking, "That was great. I'm going to do that when I get home." Before you knew it, you forgot what you've learned and stopped using your new skills. Why? Because you didn't take time for training yourself. If you are going to be a great coach, you need to set aside time to practice. Jot down the five coaching strategies and place them somewhere you look often—the bathroom mirror, the door of the fridge, the dash on your car. Every day, make time to work on one of the five skills. Before you know it, they'll be part of you. It's that easy. Whatever you practice, you get better at—just like your other family members.

# Can You Teach an Old Dog New Tricks?

It's never too early or too late to get your family working together. You've changed yourself, learned the six secrets of creating family teamwork, attended the coaching clinic to sharpen the five skills of great coaches, and now it's time to put what you have learned to the test. Are you willing to give yourself and your family members a week to make the transition? Is a seven-day plan within the realm of possibilities in your busy life? We're not saying that it only takes seven days to change, or that it always takes seven days to change. We do know that if you spend a little time each day for a week, especially with problems that have you stumped, you'll have the jump-start that can propel you forward with success.

Here's how the seven-day plan works. On day one, slow down, sit back, and assess the situation. It may not seem like much, but wait until you see what you discover by pulling back. On day two, based on your observations, decide on one thing that you'd most like to work on and formulate a plan. This is a mental exercise, not something you tell others. Day three is when you communicate the plan to the family and listen to their responses and/or resistance. By the end of the conversation, you should have something in place that you can practice for the rest of the week. Day four is time for training so you can teach family members what they need to learn to succeed. Days five and six are practice days so that the new jobs become easier for everyone. Whatever people practice, they get better at. By day seven, it's time to celebrate your progress with the family.

## THE SEVEN-DAY PLAN HELPS REVERSE LONG-ESTABLISHED PATTERNS

Ellen is the mother of three children ages sixteen, eight, and four. Her family has been very traditional, with Dad going to work each day and Mom staying home with the kids. Ellen was the most motivated to make changes and took her new job as family coach seriously. She decided to put the seven-day plan into practice.

Ellen chose Saturday when everyone was home to sit back and observe. She noticed that most of the day family members were engaged in separate activities or running back and forth from games or practices. People were in and out of the kitchen all day, grabbing snacks, leaving dishes everywhere and food spoiling on the counters. By evening, the family waited for her to begin dinner, grumbling because it wasn't ready by six and they were hungry. Ellen started dinner while the rest of the family sat in front of the TV. Her four-year-old came into the kitchen to ask her to watch him play with his toys. Her sixteen-year-old pitched a fit because she needed Ellen to iron a shirt for her date that evening. Her eight-year-old played video games while watching a basketball game on TV and reluctantly came to the table protesting that he'd rather eat in front of the game. Ellen cleaned up after dinner, ironed the shirt, threw a load of laundry into the washer, and started picking up the messes around the house. She felt exhausted and amazed at what she saw happening in her home. Even though she had been living this way forever, when she became the observer, the patterns seemed a lot clearer to her.

On Sunday, Ellen decided that she would begin making changes starting with mealtimes. She couldn't wait until Monday to communicate her ideas to the family because she was afraid they'd be too busy to take the time to listen to her and she'd have to wait till the following weekend. She wasn't sure she could go another day without help, either.

Ellen made the family's favorite brunch, chocolate chip pancakes, and called everyone to the table. When they sat down, she said, "I have something really important that I'd like to talk about. I need more help around here and I'd like to start with mealtimes." The family members gave a collective groan and went back to eating their pancakes.

Her husband, Mike, was the first to say, "I'm not doing housework. You're home all day; it's your job." The three children, following Dad's lead, chimed in, "Dad's right. You're the mom. It's your job." She remembered that it was her job to listen to resistance, so she listened without arguing. Instead of feeling put off, she asked the family if they would be willing to continue discussing their feelings with her.

Before she began to clear the table after dinner, she said, "Tell me more about why you think it's up to me to do all the work around the house. Are there reasons other than the fact that I'm the mother or that I'm home during the day? I'd like to hear your thoughts."

Four-year-old Max spoke up first. "Mom, I don't know how to cook or clean." Everyone laughed.

Then eight-year-old Kevin said, "All my friends' moms stay home and take care of everyone. Why can't you be like other moms? What if my friends came over and saw me doing dishes? That's girls' work."

"I don't have time to do any jobs at home. I'm trying to keep my grades up, I'm on the volleyball team, and my boyfriend is already complaining that he never gets to see me," sixteen-year-old Jill said.

"No wonder you're worried about changing things around here," Ellen replied. "Let me ask you a question. Do you think it's fair for one person to do all the work? Would you like to be that person?"

"Ellen," said Mike, "we aren't trying to be unfair, but you are home all day."

Rather than getting angry or defensive, Ellen responded calmly. "I can hear all the reasons it would be hard to change. Maybe if we start by listing all the jobs that need to be done around mealtime, it would be easier to see why I'm asking for help. I'm not suggesting that we divide up all the jobs equally, but I do have a lot of faith in our family and know we can come up with a solution that works for everyone."

The family agreed to make a list of jobs, and when they saw the length of the list, they were surprised at how long it was. To Ellen's surprise, they offered to pitch in and help with at least one chore. Ellen knew this was a good beginning and she thanked her family for their understanding and their help, saying, "We can start tonight at dinner. I'll post the list of what you agreed to do where you can see it. I'm sure it will take some time for us to get used to doing things differently, but if we practice all week, it might get easier."

"Max, I'll teach you how to set the table tonight. Kevin, do you need a lesson on how to make a salad? I could work with you till you feel more comfortable."

Kevin said he'd like some help, and Jill explained that she had a lot of homework, so if she was going to wash dishes, the family needed to eat early so she'd have enough time. Mike dragged his feet, but finally agreed to sweep the floor.

Ellen wanted her family to have a "can-do, we're in this together" attitude, and her discussion with the family was the beginning of a process to create that. She was a bit impatient, not wanting to let time pass before she got help, but her family was ready to assist on a limited basis and she decided to view this as progress. On Monday,

Tuesday, and Wednesday, everyone pitched in, doing the chores they agreed to do, with Ellen coaching and teaching and offering encouragement. On Thursday Ellen asked the family if they thought they could manage without her, as she was invited to a friend's house. To her surprise, everyone said fine and the kitchen was more organized than she had expected when she came home later that night. On Friday, day seven, Ellen suggested that the family celebrate their first week of chores together by ordering a pizza and watching a movie together. Jill had a date, but before she left, she said, "Next week, I'd like to switch with someone so I don't have to do dishes. How about if I cook and someone else can do the dishes?" Ellen said that maybe the family could review the list of chores the following day and everyone could try something new for the next week.

Ellen's coaching style invited allies. Even though Ellen was doing more than her share in the household, she didn't let that discourage her. Instead of continuing to wait on everyone or complain about her life, she became a coach and an organizer. She set realistic expectations because she knew that learning new skills takes time and planning. Because she focused on making changes step-by-step to win cooperation, she met with success.

One of the reasons Ellen was so successful was that she chose one task to concentrate on for a week. Working on one thing at a time works better than trying to change everything at once. Ellen also created a family work time when everyone worked together, which helped members of the family feel like a team.

## SEVEN DAYS CAN HELP YOU CHANGE YOUR TONE OF VOICE

Gretchen, a twenty-five-year-old graduate student living with three other friends, was upset with the lack of cooperation in her household, so she decided to work on the seven-day plan. She thought she was following the steps, but she wasn't getting anywhere.

One day Gretchen accidentally recorded herself complaining about the messes. Shocked at the nagging tone in her own voice, she decided to practice using a more pleasant tone. She recorded herself during her practice time and listened to the tape in her car on the way to work. In less than a week, her roommates noticed the difference and commented on how much nicer it was to be with Gretchen.

## THE SEVEN-DAY PLAN HELPS YOU LEARN TO ASK FOR WHAT YOU WANT

In another household, Steve, a single parent of two school-age children, was constantly irritated and resentful because his children acted like guests in the house. Instead of talking about this with his children, he kept doing everything himself. To change this pattern he decided to ask for what he wanted and say how he felt for thirty minutes each day.

That evening, he set the timer on the stove for a half hour before dinner, he said to his eight-year-old son, "Hey, Blake, I want some help with dinner. How about setting the table?"

"No way, Dad, I'm right in the middle of Super Mario Brothers."

"Blake, I don't like being treated like a servant. Lissie, how about you? Will you set the table or do some other job to get dinner started?"

Ten-year-old Lissie stared wide-eyed at Dad and said, "I thought you liked doing everything yourself. I didn't know you were angry. Why didn't you just ask for help?"

Steve, in shock, answered, "I thought I had."

"No, Dad, you didn't. If you ask in a nice voice, I'll help you."

After a week of practicing openness, Steve was amazed at how much Lissie was involved in family routines. Even Blake was turning his game off and watching his father and his sister. Steve decided it was worth continuing his new behavior for another week to see what would happen. He also noticed that he wasn't as angry and was actually enjoying spending time with the children.

You don't have to change everything at once. By focusing on one thing at a time, like Steve did, you can relax, knowing that you and your family are gradually learning new ways to relate, step by step.

## IN SEVEN DAYS YOU CAN LEARN TO TALK LESS AND ACT MORE

Rolanda decided to work on talking less for her seven-day plan. Her three kids didn't listen to a word she said, and after observing the situation she realized it was because she rarely followed through with action on anything she asked. Her plan was to keep her mouth shut unless she really meant what she was about to say and was ready to follow through with action. She told her kids about her plan and asked them if they would help her by giving her some kind of signal if she went back to her endless talking and barking orders. Peach, her ten-year-old, said, "Mom, how about if I put my hands over my ears if you're talking too much?" Rolanda said, "I think that would make me angry. How about if you do those talking hands you saw in the movie? That would make me laugh."

The three days set aside for practice led to some pretty interesting lessons. The first thing Rolanda realized was how much she was yelling at her kids from another room. She decided if she didn't have the energy to get out of the chair and go find them so she could have eye contact, she wasn't going to say a word. This cut down about half of her useless chatter. She also realized how much she explained herself, over and over and over. By replacing explaining with gently leading her younger children by the hand to the task they needed to do, she discovered how little her words were helping.

Finally, she discovered that if she didn't say a word, most things eventually took care of themselves. For instance, instead of chasing down her kids or clothes when the dirty clothes weren't in the laundry, she washed only the ones in the hamper. When toys remained scattered about the house after the pick-up deadline, she threw them in a box on a shelf in the closet. She was amazed that no one seemed to miss any of the toys.

Rolanda realized that she told her children her plan, and that there really wasn't a need to repeat herself. By paying closer attention to her behavior she became proactive, and realized that she could talk a lot less and act a lot more. One of the biggest changes she made was to tell her eight-year-old twin boys, Roland and Ronell, that she would let them know ten minutes before it was time to leave and then set the timer on the stove. Rolanda made sure she had their undivided attention and said, "Boys, when the timer goes off, I'll be out the door and on my way with no reminders and no nagging. I know you two can help out if you want to."

"Okay, Mom. Can we go play now?" Roland asked.

Before, Rolanda would have been tempted to explain why she needed to do this and to repeat her instructions—at least five times. Instead, that afternoon, she poked her head in the playroom door and said, "Boys, I'm setting the timer to leave for baseball practice in ten minutes." No one looked up or stopped what they were doing. Without another word, she went to the kitchen and set the timer. When it buzzed, she stuck her head in the door and said, "Time to go," and walked to the car.

Ronell ran after her saying his brother wasn't ready. Rolanda just smiled and started the engine. Her son ran back into the house and soon returned with his brother, who carried his jacket and shoes.

"Mom, you're supposed to remind us and wait for us!" Roland complained.

Rolanda continued to smile as the boys put on their seatbelts and settled in. As she backed up the car, Ronell commented to his brother, "Mom sure is acting weird. I don't think she's going to wait for us anymore if we're not ready. We better listen for the timer next time."

By day seven, Rolanda had cut her giving-orders chatter down about 80 percent. She replaced all the useless words with conversations about the kids' activities, friends, what they were doing in school, and a way they could celebrate. She said to the kids, "While we're driving around in the car, let's think of fun things to do one day a week. We could start today. Does anyone have any ideas?" Before long, the kids were throwing out choices of ways the family could play together.

Rolanda's kids were learning a valuable lesson: when Mom (or another grown-up) talks, it's a good idea to listen. They took Mom seriously because she was serious. When you use fewer words, you have more energy to enjoy yourself and your family.

## USE THE SEVEN-DAY PLAN TO INVOLVE KIDS THROUGH LIMITED CHOICES

Robert's two girls spent three days a week with him. When they left, it took him a day to clean up after them. He decided that his work was to involve the girls while they were at the house by using limited choices. His girlfriend had noticed that he was very bossy with his girls and suggested that they might respond better if they had a choice. Robert agreed and decided that he would spend some time several times a day coming up with choices.

How often have you heard a parent say, "Johnny, pick your truck up. NOW!" only to get, "No, I won't" for a reply? When you command or demand that your children, spouses, or housemates do things according to your time schedule or precisely the way you'd do it, you set the stage for a conflict. When family members believe they have no choices, they often end up engaging in power struggles. By offering limited choices, you can define the limits of a situation (your job as a coach) yet still provide freedom of choice within the boundaries. By asking, "Johnny, do you want to pick up your truck or your ball first?" you let Johnny know you expect the job will be done. But you also communicate that Johnny can choose which toy to begin with. It's important to keep choices simple and to the point.

Here are some examples that Robert worked on the three days his girls stayed with him. On Saturday morning he said, "Do you want to dust the table or the bookshelves?" His daughters, caught unawares, said, "We can dust the table."

At mealtime he asked, "Do you want to put the silverware or the plates on the table?" One of the girls said she would do the silverware while the other offered to do the plates.

Before bed, he asked, "Do you want to put your toy on the top shelf or the bottom shelf?" His six-year-old said, "Daddy, can I leave my toys out so I can play with them tomorrow?" Robert thought for a minute and said, "Would you like to put your toys away, or would you like me to put them away?" His daughters knew that if he put them away, they'd be somewhere hard to find, so they scrambled to put the toys on the shelf.

Robert also discovered how easy it was to clean up the toys if he helped the girls. He asked the girls if they'd like to clean up by themselves or with his help. They loved to clean up with him, and thought it was a great game. Robert sat on the floor with the girls, working when they worked and stopping when they stopped. Sometimes the girls would stop to see what he would do, and when he stopped, they both started laughing.

Robert was surprised at how cooperative his daughters were when they had choices. He thanked his girlfriend for the suggestion and told her how much nicer it was to be around the girls when they weren't so obstinate.

Once you offer limited choices, you don't need to repeat them. After the words comes action. If a family member gives an unacceptable third alternative, it's okay to say, "I'm sorry, that's not one of the choices." If a family member is unhappy with the way decisions are made, suggest he or she write the complaint on a list to discuss at a family meeting. (See chapter 7 for more on family meetings.)

## THE SEVEN-DAY PLAN HELPS YOU
## WORK WITH THE ECCENTRICITIES
## OF BIRTH ORDER

The world looks different depending on your birth order. Rather than getting into the complexities of this fascinating subject, our goal is to show you ways to be more encouraging to children based on their birth order position. See the Birth Order Chart to help you in this effort.

Here's how one family used birth order information to encourage all their children to help with family work. Janet and Alvin have four children. Their oldest child, Tiffany, is twelve and is very responsible. She looks after the younger children and helps with the cooking, cleaning, and yard work. When the parents started to include the younger children in the family chores, they saw a side of Tiffany they didn't know existed. She became critical, pouty, whiny, and angry. Janet and Alvin realized they had allowed Tiffany to take on too much responsibility, and the other children were acting less capable as a result.

Nine-year-old Jeffrey had convinced everyone that he was incapable of doing the chores, but after reading the Birth Order Chart, Janet realized that she had never spent any one-on-one time with him to show him how to do things. She set aside time to teach him how to fold the towels, wash lettuce in the spinner, and water the indoor plants. Jeffrey loved the special attention from his mother and was soon doing more work around the house. Whenever Tiffany saw Jeffrey helping out, she criticized and corrected him, but Jeffrey just said, "Mom showed me how to do it this way."

Six-year-old Monica disappeared whenever there was work to do. Alvin decided to help Monica be more capable. He started by asking for her help and for her opinion about how to do a particular job. "Honey," Alvin said, "do you think we should use the broom or the vacuum on the kitchen floor to pick up the dirt the dog dragged in?"

# BIRTH ORDER CHART

| POSITION | TYPICAL CHARACTERISTICS | THINGS TO DO OR SAY TO BE ENCOURAGING |
|---|---|---|
| First Child | Wants to be first and best. <br> Takes responsibility for other siblings. <br> Likely to become a high achiever, responsible. <br> Likes to be center of attention. <br> When dethroned becomes discouraged and difficult. <br> Protects, desires to be on top—superior. | Appreciate skills—"You're an expert at this," "This is your specialty." <br> Avoid pressure to be perfect. <br> Encourage the fun of participating, not the goal of winning—"We're doing this together." Teach that "mistakes are for learning." <br> Take time for training instead of assuming they have skills. <br> Give choices. <br> Ask to step back and let younger siblings do the job. <br> Pay for child care. |
| Only Child | Used to being center of attention. <br> Unsure of self in many ways. <br> May feel incompetent compared to others. <br> Likely to be responsible, achievement oriented. <br> Often refuses to cooperate if fails to get own way. | Don't treat like slaves. <br> Provide opportunities to work together with other children. <br> Have spend-the-night company. <br> Utilize child care and nursery schools. <br> Provide opportunities to participate instead of doing for them. <br> Focus on effort—not perfection. <br> Say, "I'm so glad you're helping," "I couldn't get it done alone," "Your help means a lot to me." |
| Second Child | Flexible and friendly. <br> May try to catch up with older child's competence. | Encourage his or her uniqueness. <br> Avoid comparison with oldest. <br> Say, "I need your help." |

| | |
|---|---|
| | Solicit child's input. |
| May try to be older child's opposite in many ways. | Spend time one-on-one to teach skills. |
| Not as concerned with rules. | |
| May rebel in order to find own place, feels life is unfair. | |
| Demands less attention. | |
| **Third Child** | |
| Squeezed—doesn't have the privileges of oldest or the prerogatives of youngest. | Make time for one-on-one work activities. |
| May feel crowded out, unsure of position. | Include in family work. |
| May be sensitive, bitter, or vengeful. | Ask for his or her opinion: "How can we do this?" |
| May be a good diplomat or mediator. | Listen and encourage the child to share feelings. |
| Develops particular talent to distinguish herself or himself. | Ask to step back and let younger siblings handle tasks. |
| | Give appreciation—"You really helped," "You have good ideas." |
| **Youngest Child** | |
| Often spoiled by parents and older siblings. | Do not do for the youngest (especially on a regular basis) what he or she can do alone. |
| Becomes the boss with her demands. | Don't rescue, don't pity. Say, "I know you can do this." |
| Sometimes kept a baby. | Don't refer to as "the baby." |
| Does not learn skills. | Encourage self-reliance. |
| Often self-indulgent. | Train to develop skills. |
| May be highly creative. | Provide opportunities to participate. |
| May be good at getting others to do things. | "Scale down" tools. |
| | Make it a game. |

"I don't know, Daddy, because I've never cleaned the floor. Tiffany always does that job."

"Well, Tiffany has a lot to do around here, and it's time we helped her out. Why don't you get the vacuum and I'll get the broom and we'll try an experiment to see which one works best."

"Okay, Daddy, I'll be right back," Monica said, and ran to get the vacuum. Tiffany overheard this conversation in the next room and came running to her father in tears. "I thought cleaning the floor was my job. Don't you like the way I do it?"

Alvin gave Tiffany a big hug. "Tiffany, you do everything well, and we appreciate your help, but it's time for you to let your sister and brothers learn to help. There's plenty for all of us to do. You don't want Jeffrey, Monica, and Marcus to grow up and not know how to do things, do you?"

Tiffany thought for a minute. "You're right, Dad. It's time they learned, but I knew first!"

"You sure did, Tiffany, and you'll always be our very special daughter." Tiffany sniffed back her tears as she went back to her projects.

No one expected four-year-old Marcus to do a job well. Janet and Alvin asked the other children if they would be willing to stop calling Marcus their "baby brother" and to let Marcus work with them when a job needed to be done. When it was time to pick up the toys and dishes in the living room, a family member would call for Marcus, saying, "Marcus, we need your help. Come work with us to clean the living room." Marcus would come running, because he liked to be part of the family work. Janet found a chair Marcus could stand on and she taught him how to add ingredients to salads and to take the silverware from the dishwasher and put the pieces in the silverware drawer.

Janet and Alvin noticed Tiffany correcting her siblings or complaining about their work from time to time. They would wink at her and beckon her to them, whispering in her ear, "We love you, honey, and we appreciate you helping us help your sister and brothers grow up. Would you be willing to zip your lip and let them learn without criticism? I know it's hard, but we have faith in you."

Tiffany, feeling special for being her parents' ally, winked back and said, "Okay, I'll help you out."

A different mom realized that she needed to use the seven-day plan to help her stop treating her youngest like a helpless baby. As Krista watched how everyone waited on Meg, she thought back to how old Meg's sister, Charlotte, looked when she was four and Jules was two and Meg was a newborn. Now Charlotte was eight, Jules was six, and Meg, at four, seemed like a helpless little kid. Charlotte had taken on the role of little mother, doing everything for Meg and treating her like one of her dolls. Even Jules answered for Meg and babied her.

Krista formulated a plan on day two of her seven-day changeover. She decided that she would take over Meg's training and spend time with her each day, just like she had done with each of the older children. She had allowed the other kids to become "parents," and although they meant well, they were teaching Meg to be helpless. On day three, she told the older kids that although she appreciated their help with Meg, from now on, she would spend some one-on-one time each day with Meg teaching her things. She stressed to the other children that they were great big sisters and brothers, but Meg didn't need three parents. Charlotte and Jules looked a little worried.

Krista decided to make her special time with Meg during the day when the two older children were at school. On day four, she taught Meg how to use the DustBuster to clean up the floor after lunch. Meg grinned from ear to ear as she grabbed the vacuum.

"Here, honey, let me show you how it works," Krista said. "It's easy. First push the button and the DustBuster goes on. Then push it back and forth on the floor over the crumbs. Here, you try."

Meg's expression turned serious as she pushed the button and moved the vacuum over the floor. Krista realized how much her daughter had been missing out on. The next two days she taught her how to crack eggs into a bowl and beat them with a fork to make scrambled eggs and how to empty the silverware container from the dishwasher. "Let's do this together," became her favorite phrase. Meg was at Krista's side, waiting for the next opportunity to help. She liked being able to contribute to the family.

On day seven the family celebrated Meg's new accomplishments by cooking breakfast together. Meg made the eggs, Jules set the table, Charlotte made the toast, and Mom cut flowers for a centerpiece. As the family ate their breakfast they talked about how much fun it was to see all that Meg could do, and they complimented her on the eggs. Meg felt very special.

In addition to paying attention to what special encouragement each child needs based on birth order, you may also be wondering what kinds of jobs your children can do based on their ages. Check the following lists of jobs to see if there might be something your child is ready for that you hadn't thought of.

*Tasks for two- and three-year-olds*: Pick up toys and put away, sweep the floor, vacuum, dust, set the table, help prepare meals, scrub vegetables, stir ingredients, empty waste baskets, water the plants, help clear the table, help put away groceries, put salad ingredients in a bowl, shake a small rug, help in the garden, feed pets, wipe up spills, scrub the sink and tub.

*Tasks for four-year-olds*: Set the table, help suggest items for the grocery list, feed pets, help make beds, help wash the dishes, dust, help cook, hold the mixer, empty dishwasher, put groceries away, find items at grocery store, help with yard and garden work, vacuum, load the dishwasher, make sandwiches, get cereal and milk, get the mail.

*Tasks for five-year-olds*: Help with menu planning, make sandwiches and clean up, add ingredients, scrub the sink, toilet, and tub, sort clothing for the wash, answer the telephone, take garbage out, water the plants, help with grocery shopping, pour beverages, clean room, clean mirrors, fold clean clothes and put them away, help clean out the car, help paint their room.

*Tasks for six-year-olds*: Water plants and flowers, peel vegetables, help hang clothes on clothesline, cook simple foods like tortillas or eggs, prepare own school lunch, stack wood, rake leaves, straighten and clean out drawers, take pet for a walk.

*Tasks for seven- and eight-year-olds:* Take phone messages, care for bikes, carry in grocery bags, wash down walls and floors, clean up animal messes, clean refrigerator, sweep and wash patio area, wash cat or dog, do simple ironing, fold blankets, pick berries, carry in firewood.

*Tasks for nine- and ten-year-olds:* Mop and buff floors, sew buttons, read recipes and cook meals, cut and arrange flowers in vase, help with painting, pick fruit, buy groceries for school lunches, change sheets, clean blinds, clean storage room, bake, help with barbeque, polish silver, wash car, do own laundry, clean backyard furniture, weed in garden.

*Tasks for eleven- and twelve-year-olds*: Clean stove and oven, clean pool, help build things, chop kindling, look out for younger siblings, mow the lawn, barbeque foods, run errands, stack firewood, iron.

*Tasks for teens:* See chapter 8.

Don't forget to take time for training when you introduce a new task. Pick one thing at a time, make a special time of day to teach and supervise the new skill, and work together with your children. And by day seven, you'll be celebrating, too.

# 5

# ROUTINES KEEP YOUR
# TEAM IN SHAPE

Routines have gotten a bad rap. What is the first thought you have when you hear the word *routine*? Boring! Not me! Rigid! I don't want to tie myself down. I don't do routines. My parents weren't flexible. No fun! I'm too spontaneous for routines. See what we mean? We're here to invite you to think about routines differently. Routines are more like the guardrails at the edge of a cliff or the side of a bridge. Without those stable rails, people are exposed to danger; with them, people can move about safely. Establishing routines in your family can create that kind of comfort, security, and stability.

We're also here to show you that even if you don't think you have routines, you probably do, and they may not be the ones you want. Every family has routines. A routine is doing the same thing over and over. For example, if you spend an hour trying to get your child into bed night after night after night, that's a routine. If you have to remind your kids twenty times to do what they promised, that's a routine. If you have to count to ten before anyone pays attention to you, that's also a routine. We're sure these are not the kinds of routines that you want and they certainly don't promote the kind of teamwork you're striving for.

The kinds of routines we're suggesting are the ones that improve cooperation in your family and build team spirit. The routines we're suggesting save time and energy for everyone. That's because once you set them up, they become a habit and you don't have to re-create the wheel every time the occasion reoccurs. The routines we're suggesting create independence. They also take you out of the role of boss. How is that? Because now it's *time for* bedtime, *time for* after dinner cleanup, *time for* grocery shopping, instead of "Do this because I said so!" Routines are really just habits, and like any new habit, they take a little time to get started, and then—Voila! They're a habit. Everyone knows what to do, and no one needs to think about them or organize them or worry about them once everyone is in the groove. They happen almost automatically.

Here's a prime example. One of the authors' sons was invited to dinner at a friend's house. When he came home, he said to his mother, "Mom, did you know there were families where the mom made the meal, set the table, served the food, cleared the food, *and* did the dishes? Everyone else just sat there." He had never experienced a routine like that before, because in his family, the routines were team routines, where everyone, regardless of their age, sex, or amount of extra responsibilities, chipped in and helped. If you start routines with your children when they're young, like this young man, your children will think that's just how life is. They have no experience to know it could be any different.

On the other hand, if your family is used to routines that are disrespectful, you've got your work cut out for you. They will be resistant to change, but you can do it. You have a lot of tools to use from the previous chapters. In addition to them, we'll show you some simple steps to set up routines.

## SETTING UP ROUTINES

Your best way to set up a routine is to start at the end. What do we mean by that? Picture how you'd like things to look. That's the end. If you want a great routine at bedtime, what would it look like? What time would you like the lights to be turned off and how much time would you need to make it happen? We're guessing that it would start with the kids getting in their pajamas, brushing their teeth, going to the bathroom, and then climbing into bed, waiting for you to come in and read to them or sit on the bed and talk about their day. We're guessing that a routine like that would take a half hour to forty-five minutes. Perhaps you have a slightly different picture, but you see what we mean.

Let's try again. What would the end of the routine look like if you were working on the morning routine? What time would every-one be at the door? Would all the kids be dressed, fed, shoes on, homework in backpacks, walking out the door on time for the bus, the carpool, or your ride? How much time would that take? What time would everyone need to get up to succeed? Again, it would probably take a half hour or more.

Are you getting the picture? When you start at the end, you know where you're headed. When you know where you're headed, there are a lot of ways to get there.

Let's look at a way to achieve the morning routine we suggested. Here's how setting it up looked in the Garcia family. Maria sat down with her children after school and told them that she'd like their help setting up a new morning routine. She started by saying, "I notice that you're getting better at doing things for yourself now that you're getting older. I think you're old enough to wake up and to get dressed without my help in the morning."

Maria then asked the children, "Do you have any ideas that would help you get up and dressed on time without my reminding you?" She listened to their ideas and offered some suggestions. If the children couldn't think of anything, she might have proposed the following: "Would you like to set your own alarm clock or have me set it?" "What time do you have to leave in the morning?" "What time would you have to get up to have enough time?" "Do you want to lay out your clothes the night before or pick them out in the morning?" "Would you like me to call you when breakfast is ready, or shall I set the timer?" "If you come to breakfast in your pajamas, would you like me to turn your plate upside down as a reminder to go finish or should I just tell you?"

In Maria's case, one child asked for an alarm. Another said he liked it when Maria came in and sat on the side of his bed and talked softly to him to help him wake up. The third son said that he wanted his brother to wake him up. All the kids agreed that they could get dressed and have their backpacks by the door before breakfast. They said they would brush their teeth immediately after breakfast without reminders. Manny, the eight-year-old, was very artistic, so he drew a picture of the new morning routine and Maria posted it by the kitchen table.

Maria thanked the children and suggested that if anyone forgot their agreement, she would be happy to point to Manny's picture as a reminder. Manny especially liked that idea. The family members agreed to try out the new plan the following day and then Maria asked if they would be willing to try it out for an entire school week. She reminded them that sometimes it takes time to make changes and one day might not be long enough.

For young children, charts or pictures can be fun, nonverbal reminders of routines. Charts should be simple. They are simply reminders, not scorecards. We suggest you eliminate stars and prizes as incentives. You'll find that most of your children will be happy to do the new routine when they find out they aren't in trouble if they forget.

Maria asked the children if they wanted to pretend it was morning and practice the new routine. They looked at her like she was crazy and said, "Mom, we got it. Don't worry. We'll do it." With young children, you may find that practicing in the form of putting on a play (we call this role-play) is not only fun but also extremely helpful so you can "catch" any potential problems and make sure everyone has the same picture of the plan.

For the rest of the week, Maria practiced what the family had set up, following through when needed. If someone forgot, she gently took a hand and led the child to Manny's picture, asking, "Do you see something you might have forgotten?" We call this "taking time for training." Notice that Maria did not remind or nag the children. She trusted that the kids would do what they said, and if they forgot, she led them to the chart. It worked, too. By Wednesday, the family found they had more time in the morning and were feeling a lot calmer as they started their day.

Some parents use an upside-down breakfast plate (without food on it, of course) as a reminder that part of the routine has been missed and needs to be completed before eating. If everyone agrees to this system, all you have to do is quietly check to see that the kids have done what they need to before they come to the table. If they haven't, turn their plate upside down. When your child comes to the table, usually seeing the plate is enough of a reminder to run back and complete the forgotten parts of the routine. If your child asks that you give another chance and let them come to the table with work undone, all you have to do is ask, "What was our agreement?" Your child knows what needs to be done without you nagging or reminding.

At the end of the week Maria sat down with the children to discuss how the changes were going. They all agreed mornings felt better. She than asked if they wanted to make changes, to add or subtract parts of the plan. Her daughter said it was too hard to operate her alarm clock. She and her brother decided to switch clocks.

If Maria had noticed that some of the children were wearing clothing unsuitable for the weather, she could help them pack those clothes away. When her son asked for her help picking out matching clothing, she said she'd be happy to do that before bed. He could lay out the outfit of his choice on the floor next to the bed before he went to sleep. She said she didn't want more stress in the morning, because there was enough to do and she enjoyed the time at the table with her kids.

If we look at what Maria did to set up the routine, we notice that she started at the end to get a picture of what she wanted, she talked with her kids at a relaxed time of day and asked for their help and ideas, she and the family members came up with a plan, they made a picture (you could also make a chart), she said what she would do if something was forgotten, and then she did that on the following mornings. At the end of the week, she sat with her children and evaluated how the routine went and whether they needed to make any changes the following week.

The five simple steps that Maria followed can work with any potential routine. Here they are once again.

1. Start at the end and get a picture of what you'd like to happen.
2. Involve everyone who is part of the problem at a relaxed time. Invite their help to form a routine (discuss what needs to be done and how much time is needed).
3. Make a chart or picture you can refer to and post it where all can see. Skip the stars and sticker rewards, as they aren't needed.
4. Let the plan happen. If something is forgotten, take the person to the picture/chart and ask what needs to be done.
5. Follow the plan for a limited time and then get together with the family members to evaluate how it's going and make any changes that are needed.

You can use these five steps to set up new routines for bedtime, bath time, housecleaning, shopping, cooking, laundry, packing for trips, yard work, pet care, maintaining bedrooms, dinnertime, and more. Think of a routine you'd like to have and picture how you'd like the end to look and you're on your way. Here's how another family created a dinnertime routine.

The Gregorys knew that the days of family members gathering together at the dining room table for a family meal seemed to be a thing of the past. Everyone was on different schedules and running in different directions. Like other families they knew, theirs consisted of two working parents, longer work hours, classes, practices, games, and child-care pickup, leaving little or no time for meal planning and preparation, much less eating together! As they took a step back to observe what was happening at their house, they also noticed that dinnertime was often the most chaotic time of day. The kids were cranky, they were cranky, and everyone was hungry and/or tired. Family members rushed around, making demands on everyone else in an effort to get some food together.

They were realistic enough to know that they could create some family dinners, but trying to do a dinner seven nights a week was out of the question. They believed the opportunity for family members to work together to create something that benefited the entire family was worth the effort. They also believed that when everyone pulls together, dinner takes less time to prepare and is less work.

The Gregorys were able to transform their dinnertime from chaos to the "happy hour" by following the steps outlined in setting up a routine. Evenings at the Gregorys' finds everyone in the family taking turns cooking, setting the table, feeding the pets, sweeping the floor, and doing dishes.

The first change they made was to have hors d'oeuvres—a light, healthy snack like celery and carrot sticks—to take the edge off their hunger and not spoil their appetite for dinner, while they worked together. But Mrs. Gregory knew they could do more than that, so after a week, here's what she did: On a Saturday afternoon, she sat down with her family members and told them about the problem. She said that the evenings were so chaotic and rushed and unpleasant that she hated coming home at night. Second, she asked if anyone had any ideas to solve the problem. She listened to everyone's ideas and then asked what needed to happen to have the evening meal.

Next the family members made a list of the tasks: the table needed to be set, food had to be made, the table had to be cleared, dishes and pots washed. Mrs. Gregory added that Scraps, the family cat, had to be fed and that she'd like the kitchen floor swept. They talked about when the jobs needed to happen (before or after dinner) and when they needed to start working. They also discussed what the standards would be for each job—that is, each place setting would have a plate, a fork, a knife, a spoon, and a napkin to be arranged by the setter, and so on. Next they talked about how to decide who would do which job. No one wanted to wash the dishes, so Mrs. Gregory suggested using a chart in the form of a work wheel where the jobs rotated weekly so no one got stuck with a job they didn't like doing. The kids suggested not including "sweep the floor" on the wheel and let Scraps do that job. Mrs. Gregory said she'd teach each of the children how to cook, but in the meantime, she'd do most of that and they could rotate helping cook. They agreed to evaluate how things were going the following Saturday.

Things went pretty well, although not perfectly. Once when Kevin was slow getting started setting the table, Mrs. Gregory didn't nag or yell, but instead, she calmly asked if he was going to bring the silverware or plates to the table first. By using a limited choice, she avoided inviting what could have turned into a power struggle. Another time when Amy had neglected to set the table, Mrs. Gregory started to serve the food directly onto the table. Everyone gasped and then laughed. Amy ran to get the plates and silverware and set the table.

The Gregorys also decided that meals would be served at six and if someone couldn't be at the table with the rest of the family, that was fine. Family members could eat if they liked and if not, it was okay. The family found that conversations about the food or what folks were eating made everyone uncomfortable, so they made a rule that they could talk about events of the day, world events, or other nonfood-related topics.

By using humor, limited choices, focusing on solutions, working together, and most important, by not giving up and by following through, the Gregory family had transformed their evening dinner-time and were enjoying the family "happy hour."

## SIMPLIFYING ROUTINES

With young children, you can often create a routine simply by acting and talking like the routine is how things are. Little kids accept that. For instance, you could say, "In our house we put away our toys before dinner," or "It's time for bath." Or you could say, "First we put our shoes on and then we go outside." "First/then" or "It's time" suggestions are very logical to young children.

Even with older children or all-adult households, it's okay to create a new routine by suggesting everyone try out an idea you have for awhile, assuring others that their suggestions for changes would be most welcome after the trial period. Here's how that might look. If you are the only person clearing the table and you'd like to change the routine, you could suggest at the next meal that family members form a line from table to sink and pass the dishes along. With young children, you can sing as you work. With older children, you might suggest a contest to see who can guess how long it will take to clear the table. Another possibility you could suggest would be to pass the dishes to one end of the table where one person scrapes, another stacks, and the rest carry the dishes to the kitchen.

When it's time to put toys away, start a new routine and work with the kids. Sit in the middle of the room, pick up one toy, and ask, "Where does this go?" while handing the child a toy to put away. Work as long as your child does. When the child stops, you stop. Instead of a power struggle, make it a game.

## USE DEADLINES AND ACTIVE FOLLOW-THROUGH

Another way to simplify routines is to schedule deadlines you can monitor. If you aren't present at the deadline, chances are your children will forget to follow through, and so will you. Create a deadline for every routine. When setting up a new routine, we find asking, "By when?" to establish a deadline helps family members understand the meaning of a time limit. It also helps to have an agreed, active follow-through planned so that you know what you will do if the job isn't done by the deadline. (See chapter 3.) Make sure the deadline is a time that you are available for active follow-through, as shown in the following examples.

*Before breakfast* (by when), the children should have their rooms cleaned, clothes on, and beds made. If not, you'll put their plates upside down as a reminder (active follow-through) so they can hurry and complete their task.

*Before dinner* (by when), have a ten-minute family straightening time. Gather all the family members together, set the timer, and pick up all those personal belongings, dirty dishes, and so on that have been left lying around the house. You probably spend at least ten minutes a day complaining about the messes, so remind yourself that, even though this may be inconvenient, it's a better use of your time to work with your family than to pit them against you. Imagine how effective this ten minutes can be for families where both parents get home from work after picking up kids, only to find the house in disarray.

*Before going out on Friday night* (by when), the lawn needs to be mowed. If it's not done, you'll be happy to let the friends know they can wait for the forgetful person until the job is done (active follow-through).

*Spend time once a week on Saturday morning* (by when) with each child in his or her room, helping him or her sort through the chaos. You'll be present to help your child get started if the job is overwhelming, so it can be completed before playing with friends or watching television.

Working together with a deadline helps older family members, too. Ask if someone would like company or help going through piles of collected messes. Suggest you work together before lunch on Saturday (by when) or before a Sunday outing (by when). Offer to help family members sort through their clothing to see what fits and what doesn't before the next shopping trip (by when). Help pack out-of-date items for storage or charity before returning seasonal items to the closet (by when).

With your leadership, your family can create rituals and structure that soon become part of the way things are done in your home. As family members become more proficient, they can accomplish more frequent and difficult tasks with greater ease and efficiency.

## ADDING ROUTINES AND CREATING FAMILY TRADITIONS

Perhaps family members started out helping by emptying the dishwasher before dinner. Later, they added a job after dinner, such as clearing the table. Next, they might add chores before breakfast, such as cleaning their rooms and making their lunches for school, or they can help one day a week with major housecleaning or yard work.

There are many opportunities in any household for family members to participate. Consider some of the following for your home:

Before bedtime on Sunday, water the plants. Give each person a watering container and a section of the yard or house to water. Do it together and the work will get done in no time.

On laundry day, ask for help folding towels or carrying clean clothes to the children's rooms. If the children are old enough, give them baskets of their own, put the unfolded laundry in the baskets, put the baskets in their rooms, and let them decide where to put the clean clothes. Older children can pick a laundry day and, with your help, learn to run the washer and dryer so they can do their own clothes.

Make young children their own cleaning kits: feather duster, small broom, and so on (for outdoors it might be a small shovel and a short rake) so they can work with you. Thank them for what they do. Don't complain when they leave before the job is done.

On special occasions like when company is coming, instead of sending the kids outside to get out of your hair, let them contribute to the event by finding jobs they can do. Perhaps they can make personalized place cards, put candy and nuts in bowls, make table decorations, or arrange hors d'oeuvres on a plate.

On housecleaning day, make a list of each room in the house and list all the tasks that need to be done in that room. Let family members pick the list they'd prefer. Everyone goes to the room of their choice and cleans for fifteen minutes, checking off items on the list. At the end of the fifteen minutes, if work remains to be done, family members can go as a group from room to room, finishing the lists together. Or put the list of tasks on the kitchen table and each family member picks a task, does it, and comes back and marks it done on the master chart. Cleaning is done when all the tasks are checked off.

On housecleaning day, here's a different strategy. Write each chore down on a separate sheet of paper. Put all the papers in a bag. Let each person pull three jobs out of the bag. If they don't like the job they pulled, they can trade or pull again after everyone else has had a turn.

When it's time to pack for a trip, create a master list. Pick a time of day when everyone is together. Family members can choose from the master list to get ready for the trip.

Set November as the time of year family members go through toys, games, and books. Take those that the children have outgrown or lost interest in and plan to donate them to charity. Not only will you be making room for new items and avoiding clutter but you'll also be teaching your children about helping those less fortunate.

Developing routines helps family members learn to think ahead and be more sensitive to what needs to be done. Creating family routines also takes a lot of pressure off of you, the coach. Since you no longer have to be responsible for doing everything, you can give yourself permission to relax and do things you enjoy. It really is okay to take care of yourself and be good to yourself! Put your feet up, read a book, go for a walk, play tennis, rent a video, talk to a friend, fly a kite—anything you like to do for yourself. Once routines are firmly in place, children undergo a great feeling of achievement, self-sufficiency, and relief knowing they are developing the skills to manage their lives.

# 6

# KIDS IN THE KITCHEN

If you want your kids to learn how to help in the kitchen, first, you'll need to spend some time in there yourself. As one busy, single-parent working mom said, "Surely everyone can find at least one day a week to hang out in the kitchen with their kids and have some fun."

Fun is the key word. Spending time preparing food with your children can be fun. We suspect that some of your culinary experiences to date have *not* been fun. We'd like to show you how to change that, whether you're inviting the kids to join you to make meals or snacks or school lunches.

You may be asking yourself what motivation could get you into the kitchen if you never spend time there. How about making some great memories with your children? How about creating a family fun time? How about helping your kids develop skills around cooking and nutrition? How about taking time out of the hectic schedule your family follows to hang out together creating wonderful aromas and family memories? How about saving some money? How about learning to cook together instead of running out for fast food? Fast food has become a staple for so many people, and that, coupled with a lack of physical activity, is the reason that obesity has become a national health crisis here and in many other parts of the world. (According to an article in the *St. Louis Post Dispatch* on September 25, 2004, one in three young people is overweight and one in six is obese.)

Many of you reading this book enjoy spending time in the kitchen, but perhaps haven't thought of adding your kids to the mix. We've found that in addition to the benefits already mentioned, picky eaters who seem to complain about everything you cook suddenly like to eat what they cook. In addition, when kids get to do things usually done by adults, they feel more important and grown up. As we've pointed out throughout the book, most kids start off wanting to help, so having kids in the kitchen is a great way to encourage that attitude of contribution. As children help out more, they begin to see themselves as capable, competent, contributing members of your household.

If you haven't been spending time in the kitchen, we suggest you start with one day a week to cook together. Or you could be really brave and go into the kitchen every day at five or six with the idea of putting something together that results in a family dinner by six or seven. As you become more comfortable, add your kids to this venture.

We've discovered three activities for getting kids involved that seem to work out really well. One is to let them choose the menu one night a week and be the assistant chef on those nights. Another is to obtain a kids' cookbook, complete with pictures, and invite the kids to find meals or foods that look good to them. Let them cook the item with you, or as they become more skilled, let them cook the item for the family with you being available to assist. The third technique is to involve the kids in making their school lunches.

## INVOLVING KIDS IN MENU PLANNING

All family members can have their favorite dish at least one night a week when the person who cooks gets to pick the menu. The Marker family decided to start with that idea, and told the kids that one night a week they each could choose the dinner menu and then help cook it. They created a ritual that took place on Sunday afternoons when the family sat down together and planned the week's dinner menus. Everyone in the family suggested dinner ideas, which Dad wrote on a large erasable weekly calendar. For example, Sunday night Dad would cook his famous ribs. Monday was pizza take-out. Tuesday Mom signed up to cook chicken, while Junior volunteered to make hot dogs on Wednesday. Jesse said he'd make tuna casserole on Thursday. The family members thought Friday could be "leftovers" day, and Saturday, the family would go out. Once the menus were decided, Mom made a shopping list so that all necessary ingredients would be on hand for the entire week, thus avoiding endless trips to the store or last-minute decisions to order take-out or eat fast food rather than shop for food.

Once the grocery list was completed, Mom called the family together. Each person had a piece of paper and a pen, which he or she used to write down ingredients that were needed from the store. Before they left home, someone set a stopwatch to see if they could complete the shopping in an hour. The family members piled into the car and headed to the store.

When they got there, each person grabbed a cart and took off in a different direction. About twenty minutes later, they met at the checkout counter and unloaded the groceries. Then it was home again, where all helped unload the car, put away the groceries, and fold the bags. Breathlessly, the family checked the stopwatch to see how well they did. If you are shaking your head in disbelief as you read this scenario because it seems impossible, you couldn't be farther from the truth. The Marker family created such a fun-filled event on shopping day that the kids' friends often asked to come along and help.

If this shopping trip sounds like a nightmare to you, but you'd still like to involve the kids in shopping, here are some other ideas. You could ask the children to help you by finding an item on your list— a can of fruit or a box of cereal. Another idea might be to give younger children pictures or labels on cards that they can hold. With two or three cards, they have their own shopping list and can look for specific items to match up as they go up and down the aisles. Some stores have small shopping carts so that kids can push their own carts up and down the aisles. If they can read, suggest they find the lowest priced brand or the one with the least amount of salt or fat. Show them how to read the labels so they can succeed. Not only will they help the family but they'll also learn about nutrition and develop intelligent consumer habits. As your teens get older, let them take over more responsibility, such as doing all the grocery shopping. Once teens have a driver's license, they are often eager to do errands that involve the car and give them more driving practice.

In the Johnson family, the parents were concerned about teaching the children to eat healthy foods. To help the children learn about nutrition, the parents made a poster with pictures of foods that they considered healthy. The kids could pick items from the poster for their dinner choice.

They also taught their children to "eat the rainbow," an idea their second-grader, Mindy, brought home. Mindy heard a presentation by Sonoma County, California, nutritional consultant Laurie Williams, who suggested that children need to eat a variety of different colored foods, just like the rainbow. Laurie asked the kids how much fun it would be to build something out of Legos if they only had one color. The children related to that quite easily and agreed that more colors were better. Then Laurie explained that more colors are better for growing children, too, because different foods have different vitamins and minerals that children need to have to develop and be healthy.

With her help, the children brainstormed foods that were found in nature that were red (peppers, apples, plums, etc.), foods that were yellow (bananas, pears, lemons, etc.), and so forth. Mindy brought home her school papers and showed them to her family members who decided to think of more foods from each color. They made a long list and posted it on the refrigerator. Even though Mindy was only in second grade, she was able to influence the eating patterns in her family by sharing what she had learned.

Mindy shared further information that Laurie had taught the children. She explained that it is best to eat foods as close to the way nature makes them. If you can pick something off a tree, get it from a plant, or find it in the ground, it is healthier than eating foods that have been processed. The children learned that eating an apple was healthier than drinking apple juice, or eating an orange was better for them than drinking orange juice, because the processing removed fiber and nutrients. With a serious face, seven-year-old Mindy told her family members that it was okay to drink juice, but it was better if they ate more things the way nature made them.

## USING A KID-FRIENDLY COOKBOOK

There are many ways to include kids in the kitchen that don't require much knowledge of cooking. In fact, cooking may have become a lost art. With the advent of the microwave, many people no longer need to use their ovens to cook and instead use them to store containers and bags. But since most people still enjoy eating (there are numerous cookbooks on bookstore shelves that seem to confirm this), you might want to consider cooking as a skill that would be useful for your child to have. It will certainly stand your children in good stead for their future.

If you don't have training or are out of practice in the kitchen, don't worry. If you can read, you can cook.

A good place to start is with one of the many books with simple, easy-to-follow recipes. If you'd like to learn to cook with your kids, we suggest finding cookbooks that specialize in recipes that have few ingredients and that are simple.

It will be easier to prepare meals if you have a place to work and the appropriate equipment. You don't need a lot of fancy tools. Here are some suggested basic kitchen items:

| | |
|---|---|
| a set of measuring spoons | a cutting board |
| a set of measuring cups | frying pans (both eight- and |
| a set of mixing bowls | twelve-inch) |
| a timer | saucepans with lids |
| two pot holders | a large pot |
| assorted knives | a strainer |
| a silicone scraper | paper towels |
| a wooden spoon | an apron |
| metal tongs | dish towels |
| a spatula | a casserole dish |
| a can opener | baking dishes |

To begin cooking, clear your workspace, read the recipe so you have an idea of what you will be doing, get your equipment ready, have your ingredients out and measured, and then follow your recipe.

Younger children love to help. They can peel and chop vegetables or spin a salad spinner. Older children can read the recipe aloud while you gather the ingredients from the cupboards. Measuring and using fractions is a good way for them to practice using math skills. You can cook once and eat twice by making larger portions than you need and putting the rest in the freezer (clearly marked as to item and date) for a quick healthy meal to heat up later on. Keeping a list of frozen meals on the refrigerator door makes tracking items easier.

Try something simple to take on a picnic. Make something more time consuming and let it simmer while you play a game. Teach children to use blenders and beaters to whip up a smoothie. Use large bowls to avoid overflow and provide children with special cooking aprons, mitts, or hats. Remember to have fun. Safety is an important consideration with young children and is easy to achieve with training. One of the authors had her young daughter participate as assistant chef when making the salad. She taught her how to safely cut the carrots with a sharp knife, because using a dull knife is frustrating and only makes the work harder. She learned how to hold a knife by the handle and to keep her fingers out of the way of the blade when cutting. Mom provided the necessary supervision by being there to help until her daughter became proficient.

Remember the family that was teaching their children to *eat the rainbow*, or the family that made charts of nutritious foods? Not everyone will be as concerned about nutrition as they are. Although we think that nutrition is important, we also know that involving your kids (and yourself) in cooking can be a first step that precedes learning more about what is healthy and what is not. There are many kid-friendly cookbooks that don't pay much attention to nutrition, but they certainly inspire kids to spend time in the kitchen with you. Ashley bought such a cookbook on her trip to Disney World.

Ashley didn't worry about nutrition with her kids. She figured that they would eat healthy foods part of the time, but the rest of the time, they could eat foods that she thought of as kid friendly. Her kids loved making "fish bowl Jell-O" every chance they got. Ashley purchased a goldfish bowl at the discount store. She got the idea from the Disney cookbook that had a lovely picture of gummy fish swimming in blue water—oops, Jell-O—on a bed of rocks made of cherries, grapes, and blueberries. Yes, the Jell-O had blue dye in it, and the gummy fish were filled with sugar, but Ashley thought the fun the family had far outweighed the poor nutritional value of the dessert.

On other occasions, Ashley used a cookbook that taught the kids how to make broccoli look like a tree, tofu look like a cheeseburger, and chocolate soy pudding look like the dirt in the clay flowerpot she used as the serving dish. Okay, so she did hide a few gummy worms in the soy pudding, but mostly the meal was healthy and kid friendly. Her kids loved hanging out with her in the kitchen.

Cooking breakfast can be fun, too. One of the authors remembers hearing her father say, "Breakfast is the most important meal of the day." He'd be up every morning, making her a bowl of hot cereal and a cup of hot chocolate. She wanted to provide that for her children but after reading *Children: The Challenge* (Dreikurs and Soltz 1964) and learning how capable her young children were, she realized that she'd be doing them a disservice to do for them what they were capable of doing for themselves. They could, in fact, prepare their own breakfast. The look on her two-year-old's face when she poured the cereal into her bowl and then poured in the milk from the small pitcher they had for her was indescribable.

She and her children talked and decided that she'd fix a hot breakfast two days during the week (choice of eggs or hot cereal) and on Saturday and Sunday she'd make family brunch with all the fixings. Cold cereal, breakfast bars, bagels, and shakes were available on the other days, and if anyone had the time and wanted to cook (and clean up) a hot breakfast, he or she could. She found a great breakfast cookbook and was delighted to learn that two of her children preferred cooking omelets or quiches from the book to eating cold cereal.

## KIDS IN THE KITCHEN MAKING SCHOOL LUNCHES

Mark had his kids every other week. When they were at their mom's house, she made their lunches for them. At his house, he had an assembly line lunch machine on Sunday evenings. The kids lined up at the counter and each child put one ingredient on a sandwich. Mark was last in line. He wrapped each sandwich in a plastic bag and popped it into the freezer. Each day of the week, before leaving for school, the kids grabbed a frozen sandwich, some fruit from the basket on the table, a cookie from the health food store, and some juice in a box, threw them into their lunch bag, and left for school. The entire lunch making production took about fifteen minutes on Sunday and fifteen seconds every morning.

Rob, another dad who spent time shopping and cooking with his kids, was a great fan of fitness guru Jack LaLanne. When LaLanne turned ninety, he reminded everyone of the following: You are what you eat. He said, "Would you put water in the gas tank of your car? No. It's the wrong fuel. Would you give your dog a cigarette and a donut for breakfast every morning? People think nothing of giving themselves that for breakfast, and they wonder why they don't feel good. They have no energy, and if you don't eat right and don't exercise, you won't feel good."

Rob helped his kids shop for the ingredients for their school lunches. He gave each child a budget of $2.50 for lunch treats, but also insisted that they read labels to make sure the treats had six grams or less of fat and weren't filled with sugar. Rob's deal with the kids was that they put something green, something healthy, and something new in their lunch each day, along with the snack treat. Rob knew that even if the kids traded lunches at school, they were still learning about nutrition and not spending every lunch hour eating junk food.

Mornings were too hectic for Rob's kids to make their lunches, so they decided to make them right after dinner before they started kitchen cleanup. That way, there were leftovers to recycle, time to work without stress, and only one cleanup time instead of two.

Rob realized that in some families, what people eat has become such a sore point that it has taken the joy out of food preparation and sitting down to a meal together. He didn't want to argue with his kids and ruin the joy that could come from working together to prepare foods. That didn't stop him from teaching his kids about nutrition, but he built in choices so that the kids had some power in choosing what they ate.

You can't teach your children about healthy and unhealthy eating if you don't know what you're talking about. These days, knowing what you are talking about is harder than it seems, with report after report coming out about foods that are poisonous, good for us, dangerous, artery clogging, mineral depleting, and so forth. Often, within weeks and months, someone has discovered that a food that was thought to be a bad food is now on the healthy list and vice versa. We've seen so many different diet fads come and go that we wouldn't dare promote one over another. However, once again, Laurie Williams shared some very interesting information with us that kids seem to enjoy learning. Maybe you will, too.

## FIVE FOOD GROUPS YOU NEVER READ ABOUT IN SCHOOL

Laurie introduced us to five ways of categorizing foods that make a lot of sense. There are foods that are building foods, cleansing foods, draining foods, balancing foods, and clogging foods. When she teaches children about these five groups, she suggests that when they eat, they try to figure out which group the food comes from. Then she suggests that they make sure they aren't eating too many of the draining and clogging foods.

Foods that are building foods build your tissue, which is extremely important when you are growing or using a lot of energy for work or athletics. Your body is constantly breaking down and building up, so you need protein and good fats to rebuild. A few of these foods include meats, dairy, peanut butter, healthy oils, and avocados, but this list is in no way inclusive of all the choices.

Foods that are cleansing foods help get rid of waste, help with elimination and detoxification. These foods include fresh fruits and vegetables, water, and anything that will help you flush the waste from your body.

Draining foods are those that contain no nutrients. When you eat them they not only give nothing back to your body, but they also take nutrients from the store in your body to process them, along with being a huge drain on your liver. They stress your body and leave toxins that your body can only deal with by building a reserve from eating foods that are good for you. Sugar, caffeine, artificial sweeteners, preservatives, artificial colors, drugs, alcohol, and tobacco are all draining substances.

Foods that are balancing foods are neutral and include wild rice, cooked grains, cooked vegetables, and more. They all provide vitamins, minerals, fiber, and enzymes that your body needs to flourish.

Finally, there are the clogging foods. You guessed it. They are the ones that clog your arteries, your colon, and your sinuses. They include dairy, bad fats, white bread, muffins, cookies, and most of the prepared foods you buy at the store. They build up inside your body, don't offer nutrients, and they are very difficult for your body to eliminate.

If you are intrigued and want to learn more about these five groups, we invite you to do some reading on your own and to teach yourself and your children to read labels. You can be sure that if the label has a long list of ingredients, a lot of salt, added fat and sugar, or artificial colors, flavors, and preservatives, you are eating foods that take away instead of adding to your health.

## SIMPLE RECIPES TO GET YOU STARTED

Here are some kid-friendly recipes to get you started cooking with your children. Once you begin working in the kitchen with your kids, you can add to your recipe list by using the Internet (check out www.flylady.net), cookbooks, magazines, and sharing with friends.

### French Toast

1-inch pieces of sliced bread
1 egg for every two bread slices
1/2 cup milk
1-1/2 teaspoon vanilla

1/4 cup orange juice
1 teaspoon cinnamon
spray olive oil

1. In a bowl mix the eggs, milk, vanilla, orange juice, and cinnamon. Dip bread slices into the mixture.
2. Spray a pan (nonstick) with a light film of olive oil. Place pan on medium-high heat and lift bread slices out of mixture and into pan (lower heat if necessary), turning to lightly brown all sides.
3. Remove from pan and keep warm until all slices are cooked. Serve with maple syrup or jelly.

## Cheezy Eggs

4 eggs
1 tablespoon milk
1/2 cup cubed or grated cheese
spray oil

1. Crack eggs into bowl. Add milk and beat until blended.
2. Spray pan lightly with oil. Place pan on medium heat. Add eggs and cheese and mix until eggs are firm and cheese is melted.

## Pancakes

1 cup flour
1/2 teaspoon baking soda
1/4 teaspoon salt
1 tablespoon butter, melted
1-1/4 cup buttermilk
1 egg
spray oil

1. Combine the dry ingredients.
2. Combine the butter, buttermilk, and egg. Mix into the dry ingredients.
3. Heat griddle (or fry pan), spray with oil, and pour batter in pan. Depending upon the size you want the pancakes, use a heaping tablespoon for dollar size or a small ladle for large pancakes.
4. Carefully slide spatula under pancake when browned and flip over. When second side is browned, remove from heat and serve with maple syrup or jelly.

## Banana Snacks

2 bananas sliced 1/4-inch thick
4 graham crackers

1. Put graham crackers into a plastic bag. Use a rolling pin (or mallet) to crush the crackers into crumbs.
2. Place the banana slices in the bag and shake to coat.
3. Serve.

## Egg Spiders

4 eggs
1 tablespoon mayonnaise
1 tablespoon nonfat plain yogurt
dash pepper and salt
dash Worcestershire sauce
dash dry mustard
15 large black pitted olives

1. Boil eggs until hard boiled (10 minutes).
2. Cool, peel shell off, slice in half, remove yolk, and put in bowl.
3. Mash yolks, add mayonnaise, yogurt, salt, pepper, Worcestershire sauce, and mustard, and mix together.

4. Refill hole in egg whites with mounded yolk mixture.
5. Cut olives in half lengthwise, placing one half on each yolk mound. Slice remaining halves into thin slices and arrange around yolk for legs of spider.

## Celery/Carrot Snack Sticks

2 stalks celery
2 carrots
1/4 cup peanut butter
1/4 cup ranch dressing

1. Trim ends and wash celery. Peel carrots and trim ends.
2. Slice stalks of celery into 2-inch-long pieces.
3. Cut carrots into fourths and then into 2-inch-long pieces.
4. Put one end of each stick into small bowl of either peanut butter or ranch dressing.

## Gazpacho

3 cups tomato juice
1 cup cooked corn
1 tomato, chopped
1 diced cucumber (unpeeled)
1/2 cup finely diced onion
1/8 teaspoon cayenne powder
1-1/2 tablespoon basil or 2 tablespoons chopped fresh basil leaves
3 tablespoons fresh lime juice
1/2 teaspoon salt
1/4 teaspoon pepper

1. Pour the tomato juice into a large bowl. Add the remaining ingredients.
2. Refrigerate at least one hour. Serve.

## Waldorf Salad

1 cup diced unpeeled apple
1 tablespoon lemon juice
1 cup diced celery
1/4 cup mayonnaise
dash salt
1/2 cup chopped walnuts

1. Toss apple and lemon juice. Add celery, mayonnaise, salt, and walnuts.
2. Chill and serve on lettuce.

## Grilled Cheese Sandwiches

4 slices bread
honey mustard
6 slices cheese (American or cheddar)
spray oil

1. Spread one side of each piece of bread with honey mustard.
2. Place 3 slices of cheese on one side of each sandwich. Top cheese with other piece of bread (mustard side in).
3. Spray outsides of sandwich with light film of oil.
4. Place each sandwich in a pan at medium heat. Turn over when golden. Remove from heat when second side is golden and cheese is melted.
5. Serve.

## Pizza (Boboli, Pita, or English Muffins)

1 package of 2 Boboli minicrusts or 2 pitas or 2 English muffins, split
8 oz. can tomato sauce
shredded cheese (mozzarella or jack)

1. Place the crusts on a baking pan (that will fit in the toaster oven).
2. Open the can of tomato sauce. Spread sauce on the crust. Sprinkle cheese on top to cover (you can add veggies or meat too if you like).
3. Set toaster oven to broil, put tray in, and heat until cheese is melted. Remove carefully with pot holders, as tray will be hot.

## Tuna Noodle Casserole

1 6-oz. can tuna
1 cup mixed vegetables, drained
1/2 cup milk
1/2 lb. (8 oz.) noodles
1 can cream of mushroom soup
1 clove garlic, chopped or 1/4 teaspoon garlic powder
1/2 cup bread crumbs

1. Preheat oven to 350 degrees.
2. Cook noodles as directed on package. Drain.
3. Open the can of tuna and put in bowl, breaking into pieces with fork. Add vegetables, soup, milk, and garlic to bowl. Add noodles. Transfer to a greased 2-quart casserole or baking pan. Sprinkle crumbs over the top.
4. Bake for 30 minutes.

## Chicken Pot Pie

8 oz. mixed vegetables, drained
2 cups chopped cooked chicken or turkey
1 can cream of chicken soup
1/8 cup milk
1 cup Bisquick
1/2 cup milk
1 egg

1. Heat oven to 400 degrees.
2. Mix vegetables, meat, soup, and 1/8 cup milk together in a casserole dish.
3. Stir Bisquick, remaining milk, and egg together until blended and pour over vegetable mix.
4. Bake for 30 minutes or until golden.

## Hamburgers on English Muffins

1 lb. ground beef (or turkey)
3 or 4 English muffins, split in half
ketchup

1. Divide meat into 3 or 4 equal parts. Take each section and mold into patty shape.
2. Heat pan on medium heat and place patties on pan. Cook for 4 minutes and turn over. Cook till done the way you like it (medium rare, medium).
3. Remove from heat.
4. Toast muffin halves.
5. Cut patties horizontally. Put ketchup on muffin and top each half with a patty.

## Mac 'n' Cheese

1-1/2 cup elbow macaroni
8 oz. cheese (mozzarella, cheddar, jack, Swiss, whatever you like), shredded
2 tablespoons butter
1 tablespoon olive oil
1 tablespoon flour
1 cup milk
1/4 teaspoon salt
1/8 teaspoon pepper
1/4 teaspoon Worcestershire sauce

1. Cook macaroni according to package directions.
2. Add butter and oil to saucepan and heat until butter is melted. Add flour, stirring with wooden spoon until smooth. Gradually add milk, stirring until smooth and mixture thickens. Lower heat and add cheeses, salt, and Worcestershire sauce. Remove from heat and stir until smooth.
3. Drain macaroni and add to cheese sauce. Serve.

## Hero Sandwiches

1 hero bread loaf (about 12 inches long)
assorted cold cuts of your choice (ham, turkey, salami, etc.)
assorted cheese slices (American, Swiss, jack)
lettuce leaves
tomato
pickle slices
condiments—ketchup, mayonnaise, mustard

1. Slice bread horizontally.
2. Spread mayo and mustard on both halves of bread.
3. Arrange meat slices on bottom half of bread about 2 or 3 layers thick. Arrange cheese slices on top. Arrange lettuce, pickles, and tomatoes on top and cover with top half of bread.
4. Cut into 2- or 3-inch slices.
5. Enjoy.

## Cauliflower

1 head of cauliflower
1/2 cup water
1/4 cup nonfat plain yogurt
1/4 cup mustard
4 to 5 slices cheese (American, jack, whatever you like)

1. Trim leaves off bottom of cauliflower.
2. Place in bowl, add water, cover with paper towel, and microwave for 5 to 8 minutes on high (or until cauliflower is tender).
3. Mix yogurt and mustard together.
4. Drain water from cauliflower, and then spread mixture on top of cauliflower. Place cheese slices on top to cover. Microwave for 1 minute or until cheese melts.

## Bean Sprout Salad

4 green onions
3/4 to 1 lb. bean sprouts in plastic bag
3 tablespoons sesame oil
2 tablespoons reduced-salt soy sauce

1. Trim green onions and slice into 1/8-inch pieces. Add to bag of sprouts. Microwave until tender.
2. Pour 1 tablespoon sesame oil into an empty bowl and microwave for 39 seconds.
3. Drain sprout mixture and pour into bowl with heated oil. Add rest of oil and soy sauce. Toss and serve.

## Mashed Potatoes

8 red-skin potatoes
1 teaspoon butter
1/8 cup milk
1/8 cup sour cream
1/4 teaspoon salt
1/8 teaspoon pepper
1/8 cup finely diced onion

1. Put potatoes in boiling water and boil until tender (knife sticks in easily).

2. Drain potatoes and mash. Add butter, milk, sour cream, salt, pepper, and onion and mix thoroughly.
3. For variety you can substitute 1 chopped garlic clove or 1 tablespoon of horseradish for onion.

Bon appétit!

# 7

# THE ART OF GROUP
# DECISION MAKING

A young woman watched a mother and her elementary school–age daughter prepare to order from a restaurant menu. The mother asked the child what she wanted and discussed her preferences at length before ordering. The woman watching had been raised in a family where no one ever asked children what they thought. As she relayed her story to one of the authors, she said in amazement, "Can you imagine growing up in a family where people actually talked to each other?"

We can imagine, and so can you. By now, if you have been practicing the ideas in this book, you've had many conversations with your children and even experienced those magic moments watching your children do better when they are listened to and taken seriously. Research has shown that children who learn to think through the consequences of their decisions have better self-esteem, and that children who are involved in decision making treat others with more respect. That's why we are focusing on the skills for conversation in this chapter. In the following stories, notice how even very young children grasp the idea of talking things out.

Three-year-old Jake got angry when his four-year-old cousin Patti kept knocking down his fort. Several times he asked Patti to stop, but she didn't listen. Finally, Jake grabbed Patti's hand, pulled her toward his little table, and said, "Patti, we need to have a meeting."

Jake lives in a family that holds regular family meetings, and at age three, he knows the way to solve problems is to talk about them at a meeting. Many children his age solve problems by hitting, kicking, biting, crying, or tattling to a parent. Jake has already learned better tools for conflict resolution.

Two-year-old Ellie is learning from her parents, Ted and Gita, that her opinions are important. Whenever she says no, her parents say, "Let's talk about it a little first." Then they ask Ellie what she wants, say how they feel, and offer Ellie limited choices. Ted and Gita realized Ellie was catching on to negotiation skills one night when Ted said, "Come on, Ellie, time for bed." Ellie pursed her lips, looked Ted in the eye, and said, "Talky little."

These families are raising children to think and have opinions. They empower and encourage them by providing opportunities to learn respectful decision making. They focus on building their children's skills because they see the family as a place filled with opportunities to teach children skills to make their lives work better.

## ONE STEP AT A TIME

You can enhance your skills for conversation with your children, encourage them to express feelings and opinions, and be involved in solving problems by small steps, medium steps, and big steps.

### Small Steps

The following suggestions are small steps:

1. Ask your children what they think at least once a day and listen to their responses. For instance, ask, "What do you think you could do to help the family get ready for dinner?" If your child answers, "I could make decorations," don't jump in with, "That's not what I meant." Seriously consider what your child says before you respond. If your child always responds with the same idea, you could say, "I know you love making decorations, but today we need help with either carrying the plates to the table or putting the napkins and silverware by the plates. Which would you like?"

2. Offer a limited choice whenever possible. "Would you like to bring the silverware or the plates to the table?" or "Would you like to feed the dog before dinner or after dinner?"

3. Help young children think about the consequences of their behavior by asking, "If you were the mommy or the daddy, what would you do when your child does this?" Two young boys volunteered to rake the leaves and stopped after raking only a fraction of the yard. Their father asked, "If you were the dad, what would you do about the job your sons just did?" The boys grinned sheepishly and said, "We'd ask the boys to finish."

4. As your children get older, spend time each day asking how things are going and listen to what they say. This is a simple way to become aware of your children's opinions and thought processes. One family asks a question each night at the dinner table, like "What was the most embarrassing moment of your day?" or "What made you the angriest/happiest today?" Everyone in the family takes a turn answering, and all have fun sharing and listening.

5. Don't ask your children if they would like to do something if the answer "no" is unacceptable. "Would you be willing to take your little brother with you to the park?" is a request, not a command, so be sure it is acceptable to hear no for an answer. If not,

say, "I'd like your help. Please take your little brother to the park so I can get some things done without any interruptions."

## Medium Steps

Medium steps allow and encourage your children to find solutions to problems with each other without your input. By giving the children a chance to problem solve without your advice, you can find out what their abilities are, as well as enjoy some simple solutions to complex problems.

*Allow Your Children to Work Out Solutions Whenever Possible*

If you think your responsibility is to fix everything and that you are the only one with good ideas, notice how creative the children are in the following examples. They came up with inventive solutions to difficult problems with no input from their parents.

The Swanson children were fighting over whose night it was for the dishes. Their mother, Andrea, said, "I'm tired of hearing you argue every night. I'll bet you five dollars you can't figure out a way to solve this problem without fighting."

Her children looked at her in amazement. Then one asked, "Five dollars apiece, or do we have to share it?"

"I'm so sure you can't figure out a better way that I'm willing to bet five dollars each," Andrea said with a grin.

The children retreated to the living room and were back in less than five minutes to collect their money. "Mom, we figured it out. We divided the dishes into two parts and we'll do the dishes together every night. We'll take turns doing 'first part' and 'second part.'"

"Do I need to know what's in the 'first part' and the 'second part?'" asked Andrea.

"Just watch and see how well our idea will work. We figured it out and we're not going to argue about dishes any more. Can we have our five dollars?"

"How about trying your idea out for the rest of the week to make sure it works. Then I'll give you the money." By the end of the week, Andrea Swanson was congratulating herself on the best ten-dollar bet she ever lost.

In another family, the children were fighting over the new popcorn popper. Their father unplugged the unit and said, "When you've worked out a way to use the popper without fighting, you can try again."

At first the children grumbled, but later one said, "We worked it out. John can make the popcorn on Mondays and Wednesdays and I get it on Tuesdays and Thursdays. Friday is free day. We both agreed."

If the children start squabbling again, Dad can put the popper away and say, "The plan seems to be falling apart. Try again. Let me know when your plan is worked out so you can use the popper."

Sometimes children will come up with a totally new plan to get things done. In a family where everyone did the gardening and watering together, one child volunteered to mow the lawn every week if he didn't have to do any other yard work. Everyone in the family was tired of listening to his complaining, so they agreed to try the new plan for a month. When the family sat down to evaluate at the end of the month, everyone had noticed much less grumbling and hassling over yard work and was pleased with the way things worked.

Another group of children helped solve a forgetfulness problem by suggesting that each child have a tag with their job list on one side and their picture on the other. The children agreed to check their tags before dinner. When their jobs were completed, they would turn the tags over to their picture and go to dinner. If their jobs weren't completed, they would do them before going to the table. One parent looked at each tag before dinner to see whether a smiling face or a list of chores stared back. If the parent noticed a list, he or she called to the child, "Come here and show me your smiling face." Everyone knew that was the signal to get to work and complete agreed-upon jobs.

A family of five children solved the laundry room chaos by deciding to each pick a day to do laundry. They all agreed that if a brother or sister forgot the wash in either the washer or dryer, the next person using the laundry room would put the forgotten laundry in a plastic bag and set it outside that sibling's bedroom door. The parents were thrilled with the suggesion, which ended the squabbles among the children and eliminated piles of dirty clothes in the laundry room.

Even though children can solve many problems without adult interference, they sometimes need adult help. If you are having trouble with recurring problems, another medium step is to help your children solve difficulties by having a conversation. First you listen to their feelings. Then you ask if they'd like to know what you think. If they say yes, which they usually will, share your feelings. If it's necessary, you can work together to come up with a plan you all can live with. If they say no, respect that and wait a day or so, then try again.

### Listen and Share Feelings to Find Win/Win Solutions

Feelings give important information about why problems are occurring. If your children are angry or resentful, listening to their feelings can help you and them move beyond a stuck place. Usually the tendency is to try to fix people's feelings, stop them from having feelings, or tell them they shouldn't feel that way. Instead, we know that when you listen to your children's feelings, you communicate that feeling the way they feel and thinking the way they think is okay. You are practicing unconditional love and acceptance when you let your children know you hear and understand their feelings without finding fault, explaining away their feelings, or fixing things for them. Amazingly, once expressed and heard, the feelings seem to dissipate all on their own.

Your children may struggle when they first try expressing feelings. They'll use statements that include the words *like, that, as if, you,* or *they* following the word *feel.* These words indicate what they are thinking, but not how they are feeling. For example, "I feel like I can't do anything right" is a thought, not a feeling. "I feel discouraged" expresses a feeling about not being able to do anything right. A helpful hint: feelings are usually just one word: sad, angry, excited, content, overwhelmed, and so on.

Help your children express feelings by listening to what they tell you and reflecting back the contents as you fill in these blanks:

"You feel _____ because _____ and you wish _____." Since people often have difficulty with a "feeling vocabulary," in our offices, we use laminated feeling faces with feeling words to match to help them out. It isn't unusual for a child or an adult to shuffle through the faces and pick the ones that match their mood.

Eight-year-old Marguerite complained to her father that two-year-old Cassie was spoiled and not doing things the way she was supposed to. She objected to the way Cassie set the table, with silverware in the wrong place and the napkin covering the entire place setting. Marguerite said she would get in trouble if she set the table that way, but everyone laughed when Cassie did it.

Instead of arguing or invalidating Marguerite's feelings, her father said, "You're feeling upset because we laugh when Cassie does things wrong and when you make a mistake, you get in trouble, and you wish we would correct Cassie, too."

Marguerite looked at her father with surprise and said, "No, I don't want Cassie to get in trouble. She's only two. But I wish you would laugh at me the way you do Cassie."

"Oh, honey, are you jealous that Cassie gets a lot of attention?" asked Dad.

"Everyone thinks she's so cute and treats her like a baby. I wish she wasn't so spoiled."

Her father tried again. "You're feeling hurt because Cassie gets away with things and you're expected to act like a grownup and you wish we would stop spoiling Cassie."

"Yes," said Marguerite. "How is Cassie ever going to learn to do things the right way? When I was two, I couldn't put the napkin on top of the plate."

"Sweetheart, would you like to hear a story about you when you were two?"

Marguerite was intrigued and said, "Tell me what I did when I was two."

"You had a very special way of setting the table. We made a shelf just for you that you could reach, with all the dishes and silverware on it. At least ten times a day, you used to set the plates on the chairs, put the silverware on the plates, and sit on the floor and pretend you were eating. Then you would call Mommy and me over and tell us to sit on the floor with you. Then you would instruct us to eat everything on our plates. You were such a cutie!"

Marguerite smiled as she heard the story. "Did I really do that? Maybe Cassie will grow up and learn to set the table right when she's my age."

"Yes, honey, I think that will happen just like it did for you. But if Mommy and I are scolding you for making a mistake, you can tell us that your feelings are hurt. I'm sorry if I said something that hurt your feelings."

"It's okay, Daddy," said Marguerite, as she went off to play with her toys.

In another family, Mrs. Talivera argued daily with her six-year-old daughter, Amelia, about her messy room. When asked to clean her room, Amelia had a tantrum, so Mrs. Talivera decided to try listening to her daughter's feelings. She said, "You're feeling angry because it is too hard to clean this mess alone, and you wish I would help you?" Amelia corrected her and said, "I'm not angry, I'm tired, and I don't want to clean my room right now."

At this point, Mrs. Talivera decided to let Amelia know how she was feeling by using the same formula: "I understand that you are tired and would like to wait till later. Perhaps we could do that, but I have another problem. I feel upset because we are fighting, and I wish we could figure out a way to work this out without fighting."

"Well," her six-year-old said, "you always want me to clean my room when I'm tired."

"You're upset because I pick a bad time for you to clean your room, and you wish I would ask when you aren't tired?" queried Mrs. Talivera.

"Yes, and I don't like it when you yell at me either."

"Would you like to work out a plan so you can do your room when you're not tired and I can stop yelling? That would make me happy, too, because I don't like to fight with you. If we wait too long, your room will get so messy that it will be too hard to clean. I wonder if cleaning your room right before dinner might work better. Are you tired then?"

"No, I'm hungry."

"Maybe I could let you know when it's fifteen minutes before dinner. We could set the timer and you could clean your room then. Right before we sit down to eat, you could come and get me and show me your room. If you need help, I could spend a few minutes before dinner with the parts that are too hard for you. Would you like to try this out today?"

"Okay, Mom, but no yelling," said Amelia, as she gave her mother a big hug.

Amelia's mother practiced a simple problem-solving method with her child. First she listened to her child's feelings. Next she shared how she felt. Finally she made a suggestion and asked if they could try it out for a short time. If Amelia had given a different suggestion, Mrs. Talivera might have started a list of ideas and suggested they pick one to try for a few days. Finding a solution both people can live with, based on information gained by listening to feelings, is an easy way to come up with win/win solutions.

## Big Steps

### Hold Regular Family Talk Times or Family Meetings

Holding a weekly, regularly scheduled family talk time or instituting family meetings are big steps that improve communication and raise self-esteem. A family talk time is a time set aside once a week where family members sit down together and talk about whatever is on their minds. They may balk at the notion of something called a "meeting" or even something with the word "family" in it, especially if they are living in a stepparent situation, but they don't mind having a talk time. On the other hand, at a family meeting, the procedure is more formalized. Most family meetings have an agenda, usually consisting of appreciations, old business, problem solving, scheduling, and a fun activity together. Both meetings are a time for family members to air feelings, get compliments, and have conversations.

Both family talk times and family meetings should be held once a week on the same day for everyone living in the house. Make sure there are no other distractions, such as TV or phone calls. Sit around a table or in the living room. If a family member chooses not to be involved, hold the get-together without them and let them know they are welcome to join at any time. Set a time limit for your meeting from fifteen minutes to a half hour. Items not completed can be handled at the next family meeting.

During the week, post an agenda. A good place is on the refrigerator where everyone can see and write on it. Use the agenda as a reminder list for issues that are important to discuss that might be forgotten by the day you hold your meeting. In addition to serving as a reminder, the posted agenda allows you to postpone dealing with an issue until everyone is present to help solve the problem and figure out what to do.

Start each family meeting with compliments and appreciations so everyone gets an opportunity to say and hear something positive. Depending on the age and skill level of family members, you can take turns leading the meeting and writing down agreements made. After compliments, the chairperson calls off items on the agenda and helps family members take turns practicing respectful communication. The easiest way to do this is to go around the table twice, giving each person two turns to state his or her opinion or feelings about the issue without being interrupted. If the person has nothing to say, it's okay to say "I pass." This is a good time to practice the problem-solving skills in this chapter, including asking family members for their opinions, sharing and listening to feelings, and offering choices.

It is important that everyone in the family agrees before a change is carried out. This agreement is called consensus. Until you reach consensus, you might have to live with things the way they are. Some subjects need to be discussed for several weeks before a family can come to consensus. Holding a conversation without having to fix anything is a great tool for bringing about family cooperation and harmony.

Brainstorming (generating a list of suggestions without evaluation) creates more choices everyone can consider. Instead of seeking a perfect solution, suggest that family members choose one idea from the list of brainstormed suggestions to try for a short time, like one week. Set a time to meet again to evaluate the solution and discuss what everyone learned by trying it out.

Family meetings work best when everyone focuses on solutions rather than problems and who is to blame for them. No one should be in trouble at a family meeting and everyone should be listened to and taken seriously. We recommend using family meetings to discuss items of interest to the children before jumping in to solve the family chore problems. Once family members have practiced listening to and helping each other, you will have an easier time working out the details for family chores.

*Create a Plan for Sharing Chores*

If you wish to use a family meeting to create a plan for sharing household chores, try the following suggestions, which work for many families and are variations on the steps for setting up routines you read about in chapter 5:

1. Let everyone know you need help.
2. Ask what work must be done for the family to function smoothly. Write down all tasks even if they seem silly. Don't worry about missing a few.

3. Ask if each person would be willing to pick one to three things to do for one week.

4. Decide when and how often each job needs to be done and set a deadline (by when) for finishing it.

5. Create and post a chart with the information.

6. Have the person previously responsible for each job train the new person.

7. Assign one family member to check the chart each day to be sure the job is completed by the deadline. If the job is not done, this person is responsible for telling the person it is time to complete the job. It is best that the job of reminding be given to a child or to the less involved parent.

Although we may have mentioned some of these ideas in previous chapters, they bear repeating because they work so well. Don't try to get all the jobs assigned at once. Overwhelming everyone with tasks would make winning cooperation difficult. Since this is just for one week, you can make changes and add more jobs later.

Another way to share chores is to ask family members to list jobs that need to be done. Write each job suggested on a small slip of paper, put the paper into a bag, and ask each person to pick one to three jobs for the week.

With young children, you can use the family meeting to choose a time of day everyone can help each other with chores. Then together create a chore wheel that you can rotate each day to assign one job for each family member. Plan and work when everyone is present.

If family members think one person should do everything, appeal to their sense of fairness by asking, "Who thinks it's fair for one person to do all the work? Who wants to do all the work? I don't, so I'd like us to work together."

In one family meeting, the family solved the problem of housecleaning by agreeing to clean the house together once a week. Since the mom did most of the cleaning up to that point, she suggested that she list the tasks in each room and teach the rest of the family how to do each part. The family members decided to have each person clean two rooms of the house and work together. Mom agreed to assist until everyone felt competent to do the tasks without her help. The family decided to pay themselves for their work and use the money for family outings. By working together as a family, what used to be drudgery for one became a relatively easy job for many. It took the family less than an hour a week to make the house sparkle.

Another family made a list of chores to put on the kitchen table every morning. During the week, family members completed jobs when they had time and marked them off. Weekly cleaning was finished when all the jobs were marked off.

In another family, Dad wrote all the jobs on slips of paper and put them in a bag. Included on the slips of paper were some items like "Go outside and sing a funny song" or "Rest for five minutes." Each family member did the assigned job he or she pulled out of the bag, including the "fun" things.

If someone complains that he or she is doing too much or someone else isn't doing a job properly, put the problem on the agenda to discuss at the family meeting. If you think that family members can do more chores or that it's time to switch jobs, put those items on the agenda. Be willing to change your system if it's not working. Don't get locked into something your family doesn't like even after they've tried it for a while. If something isn't working, wait until the next regularly scheduled family meeting to discuss the problems and brainstorm alternatives. Waiting a week to change things might allow time to solve a problem, as family members are capable of learning from mistakes.

The Franklins used a family meeting to solve the fighting over who got to sit in the front seat of the car. Both mother and father were tired of the squabbling. The family brainstormed ideas and chose the suggestion that one person sit in the front seat on the way to the activity, the other person on the way back. Eleven-year-old Matt said he would ride in the front on the way to the destination, and Dora, age nine, said she would ride in the front on the way home. The family agreed to try the idea for a week.

At the end of the first week, Matt put the item back on the agenda. He complained that Dora got to ride in the front seat longer because of the car pool schedule. Most of the trips in his car were on the way home, and he didn't think it was fair that he got stuck in the backseat. Mrs. Franklin said that she was also disappointed in the new plan because there was still a lot of fighting in the car over who sat where. She thought it would be best to have both children sit in the back until the family solved the problem. Matt protested again, saying Dora had a whole week in the front, and now he would get even less time. The meeting ended without a solution, but everyone agreed to continue thinking of options.

At the third week, Dora put the item on the agenda. She and Matt had figured out a solution for sharing the front seat that they would like to try.

"What did you work out?" asked Mr. Franklin.

"I'll sit in the front on odd days and Matt will sit in the front on the even days unless we are going on a vacation. Then we'll count the number of days we'll be away and take turns. If it is an uneven number, one of us will get the front in the morning and the other one in the afternoon. We also decided we get the front seat on our birthday," Dora reported.

"Wow, that sounds complicated. I don't think I can keep that straight," said Mom.

"Don't worry," chimed in Matt, "if we start fighting, just tell us to sit in the backseat for a day and then let us try again. We know the plan. Right, Dora?"

"Yes, and we both agreed," said Dora.

Everyone decided to go with the new plan, which worked without a hitch for years. By using the family meeting to discuss issues, listen to feelings, and reach consensus, most problems can be solved.

Occasionally, family members refuse to cooperate or help with anything. Using the methods in this book should prevent this, but if there is a complete breakdown of respect in your situation, you may need to "take a vacation."

## WHEN CONVERSATIONS FAIL, GO ON "VACATION"

There are times when you may not be able to win cooperation in spite of your best coaching efforts. That could be a sign that you need a "little vacation." Use the six steps to winning family cooperation (p. 12) before you take action. It's still true that the family is a team and you're the coach (steps 1 and 2), but for some reason, you've ended up on opposite sides. Your goal is to get back on the same side. When you step back and slow down (step 3), you might even notice what has happened that created the problem. If you don't, it's okay. The idea is to take your time deciding what you will or will not do. Thinking through what you will do instead of barking out something you will regret or not follow through on later is a way to cool off and become proactive. As you focus your attention (step 4), you might decide that at this time the best you can hope for is to take care of only your needs—prepare food for yourself, make your bed, clean your clothes, put dirty pots and pans in a soapy bucket, keep a clean pan to use for your meals, and so on, but stop taking care of the other household members' needs. When you have a conversation (step 5), it might be a bit one-sided, sounding something like this.

"I'm going to be taking a little vacation from chores for a while because we're not on the same side, and we can't seem to get there. I can't seem to figure out why everyone is refusing to help around here, and I don't want to fight or nag about it. But it's also not respectful that I do all the work, so I'll take care of my needs for a while and the rest of you can take care of your own. Although I'll be on 'vacation,' I'm willing to listen to any ideas you might have to help us get back on the same side."

If you take this drastic step, be prepared for the disorganization and chaos that will follow. After letting the household members know what you're doing, follow through (step 6) while maintaining a friendly yet firm attitude. Don't cave in when your fifteen-year-old pleads that she has nothing clean to wear to the dance and her life will be ruined. Reply in a sincere and friendly tone that you're not going to do the wash or lend her your clothes even though you know how hard this must be for her. After experiencing the discomfort of chaos for a few days, most household members are willing to come together and discuss what changes need to take place. When this happens, remember to use the coaching strategies from chapter 3, which include valuing differences, inviting participation, using encouraging words, holding others accountable, and teaching skills.

One household experienced the effects of a vacation for six weeks before cooperation was restored. This was not a family who had been using the ideas in this book. If the parent had used the small, medium, and large steps we've shared in this chapter, it would be unlikely to come to the point where a "vacation" would last that long. As we stress throughout this book, people usually want to pitch in when they know they have a choice.

Whether using the small, medium, or big steps described in this chapter, keep in mind that the emphasis is on working things out instead of finding fault and pointing fingers. If your efforts seem to be breaking down, check your behavior to make sure you are doing more listening than talking. By leaving room for input from others, your family will run a lot more smoothly. It might also help to review the seven signs of a lack of cooperation found in chapter 2, and take measures to change your behavior to correct the situation.

# 8

# GETTING TEENS TO PLAY
# ON THE TEAM

It seems curious that a person who looks so much like an adult could act so much like a young child. We're talking, of course, about teenagers. It's particularly difficult to get cooperation from teens (sometimes known as beings from another planet). That's because helping the family is seldom high on a teen's list of priorities. In fact, family chores may not be on a teen's list at all. You may even wonder if your adolescent is still part of the household, as he or she spends more and more time away from home and is often too preoccupied to count on even when home. Of course, you are still concerned about getting help with the family chores, which haven't diminished just because the child living with you has transformed into an adolescent. As a matter of fact, sometimes messes increase after friends have dropped by. And the more you want help, the less help you seem to get. If you get angry and try to motivate your teen while under the influence of anger, you only invite power struggles and rebellion instead of cooperation. You and your teen get better at fighting rather than accomplishing anything constructive around the house.

Your teenager is at that difficult time between childhood and adulthood when your child's behavior is more of an indicator of adolescence than chronological age.

If you aren't sure whether you are dealing with an adolescent, ask yourself the following questions:

- Is your child more concerned with friends and self than with family?
- Does your child seem selfish, self-centered, and irresponsible?
- Is your child alternately very nice and very moody?
- Would your child rather talk on the phone, listen to music, or stay in his or her room than be with the rest of the family?
- Does your child complain about your nagging when you think you are making simple requests?
- Does your child suddenly get inspired to do the work, only to revert to a state of lethargy for days on end?

If you can answer yes to any of these questions, chances are you are dealing with a teenager. In that case, much of what used to work in the past will now be ineffective. There is hope for cooperation, but you'll need to change your coaching methods. We recommend the following:

1. Make room for differences.
2. Use your sense of humor.
3. Be sensitive to the needs of the "untrained worker."
4. Be creative and change what isn't working.
5. Practice joint problem solving, create mutually agreed-upon deadlines (by when), and use active follow-through.

6. Loosen the reins and encourage more adult responsibilities, including work outside the home and caring for a vehicle.
7. Tap into teenage humanitarianism.

You've come across information about many of these suggestions in other chapters, but here we'll show you how they apply to teens.

## MAKE ROOM FOR DIFFERENCES

Are you a person who cleans the kitchen as you cook or a person who leaves the mess until later? You probably have your own style for accomplishing things. If you expect your teen to do things your way, odds are that won't happen. Why not? Because your teen is in the process of defining how he or she is different from you. Since the obvious way to be different is to do the opposite, insisting that things be done your way is asking for trouble.

The biggest mistake that parents of adolescents make is taking their teen's behavior personally. Your teen sees the world through a very different filter than you do. Chores are probably not on his or her list of important issues. Remember when you were a teen? Did you fret over messy floors, unwashed clothes, dirty dishes? Probably not. Did it take your folks ten reminders before you mowed the lawn? Quite possibly. Weren't you thinking more about being popular, not being popular, fitting in, zits, making the team, or having friends than whether or not it was your turn to do the dishes?

Your teen still lives at home and is still part of the family, at least in your eyes, so it is okay to expect your son or daughter to pitch in. But if you expect teens to have your standards, you're engaging in magical thinking. We're suggesting that you lower your expectations a bit and pick your battles. Are you sure that it is more important to have the dishes lined up by height in the dishwasher than to have the dishes *in* the dishwasher? Are you really going to make a big deal out of a mop left in the bucket if the floor actually got washed without you nagging?

Sometimes it helps to talk about and agree on standards with your teens before they start a job. Keep in mind that your teen is sensitive to your tone of voice and facial expressions. A sharp or sarcastic tone with an angry scowl won't invite cooperation, even though it may reflect how you feel inside. Just because you talked about something in advance doesn't guarantee that your teen was actually listening carefully or taking the conversation seriously. Remember, teens are very distracted by what is important to them. In some ways, although they look bigger and older, they seem to act more like they did when they were toddlers. This is normal; don't despair. It doesn't last forever, either.

If you think your teen is intentionally doing poor work, instead of criticizing, ask your teen whether the job meets his or her standards. If your teen feels satisfied with the work, allow yourself to consider a different standard of cleanliness. If you think your teen is taking advantage of you, say: "Try again, I think you can do better," "The job isn't done. Please finish it," or "What was our agreement?"

One of the most volatile issues with teens is the condition of their rooms. Even the neatest child lives in chaos at some point during the teen years. Make allowances for your differences and don't make rooms an issue. Allow your children to decorate and set the standard of cleanliness for their rooms so they have a bit of the universe to control. If the room offends you, ask your teen to keep the door closed or close it yourself when you walk by. You might make an agreement with your teen that chaos is fine during the week, if once a week the room gets vacuumed and dusted, the bedding is changed, and the dirty dishes are returned to the kitchen. When you stop fighting over rooms, teens are more likely to cooperate with work in other parts of the house.

Be flexible when your teen has friends over and doesn't get things done according to the regular schedule. Unless it is a genuine inconvenience to you or other family members, relax and trust your teen to do what needs to be done once their friends leave.

Teens think you are nagging when you talk about problems that might happen, such as telling a teen he might forget to do his chores if he doesn't do them at the agreed-upon time. A teen is more apt to work with you if he or she can see that there really is a problem and if you say what your issues are. A fifteen-year-old boy was informed that he consistently forgot his chores when his friends were over and didn't do them later on his own. He asked his mother why that was a problem, and she said, "I can't concentrate or work in a mess so I have to wait for you or do your job for you before I can get started with my work."

Her son looked at his mother as if she came from another planet and said, "I didn't know you felt that way. How about this? If I don't do my work before my friends arrive, I'll ask them to help or listen to music in my room until I'm finished?"

His mother thanked him for his consideration of her feelings and said, "That would work just fine."

When her son left the room, she called her friend to get a reality check. "Janet," she said, "Am I losing my mind? I could swear I've talked to Ralph at least a hundred times about forgetting to finish his work when his friends are over, and all he does is get defensive. This time I explained why it was a problem for me, and he initiated a solution without any prodding. What happened?"

Janet couldn't stop laughing. "Sue, don't you know that teens don't like to do things because you say so, but they love to help you out with your problems? I think you've lost your sense of humor with Ralph and are taking him too seriously. You think everything he does is meant to get you, but I don't think you're really all that important in his life right now. Don't get me wrong. He loves you, but his head is elsewhere. Remember when we were that age? I don't recall thinking about our parents twenty-four hours a day. Get a grip!"

"Thanks for the dose of reality, Janet. You're right, I am too serious. Somewhere along the line, I'm afraid I lost my perspective along with my sense of humor." Using a sense of humor is one of the most effective tools for creating cooperation and harmony with a teen. If you've lost your sense of humor like Sue did, read on.

## USE YOUR SENSE OF HUMOR

Remember when your four-year-old dressed like a superhero to go to the grocery store and your three-year-old insisted on having the crust cut off his sandwiches before he would eat them? You probably thought your child was adorable. Maybe you even took a picture for your photo album or called a relative to tell stories about how precious your little one was. Now that same child is behaving in age-appropriate ways (for a teenager) and you are considering sending him to live with a distant relative instead of laughing at his uniqueness, which is different from laughing at him. What happened to your sense of humor? If you can get it back, you can make the teen years a lot more fun for everyone.

Teenagers enjoy a sense of humor and respond to it much better than to lectures and nagging. The following situations illustrate how parents used humor to invite cooperation and to lighten things up.

In one family, Mom lost her sense of humor during menu planning because she thought the family members weren't taking things seriously. One of her teens imitated her trying to save money by planning meals from available ingredients. Her son looked over the staples in the cupboard and said, "Now we have a lot of popcorn, paper towels, and rice left, so Dad, why don't you make a rice, popcorn, and paper towel casserole tonight?" Mom laughed along with everyone.

In another family, Peter, father of three teens, used betting and guessing games to motivate his children and add humor to a situation. When Peter noticed the chores weren't getting done as agreed, he'd say, "Someone forgot to do something they agreed to. I'll give a dollar to the first person who guesses what it is." The teens ran around the house trying to find what hadn't been done so they could win the dollar. Another time Peter said, "I'll bet two dollars you can't finish your yard work before the football game starts." His bets and games were effective because they were used infrequently and unexpectedly. Had Peter used bets as rewards and bribes, he would have inferred the only reason his teens helped the family was for the money, and they wouldn't have felt respected.

One day at the grocery store, in the same spirit of fun, Peter tore the shopping list in half and gave one part to his son and the other to his friend. "I'll take you two for pizza if you can find everything on your half of the list in fifteen minutes. Go!" Shoppers watched in surprise as the two teens ran through the store tossing items into their carts.

Sometimes a sense of humor is the only way to get things done. When Sharon's fifteen-year-old stepson, Cole, moved in with the family, it wasn't long before his presence was felt in the household. First her hairbrush disappeared, then half the kitchen towels, and finally several blankets vanished. He paced, twisted, twirled, and danced as he talked on the phone until the cord became a tangle of knots. Cole left his dirty dishes, magazines, and soda cans in Sharon's bedroom, where he lay on her bed to watch TV each day after school because his own room was too messy. The final straw came when Sharon started to set the table and couldn't find any silverware in the drawer, and the kitchen scissors she used to cut up some spices were missing.

"Cole Peter Anderson," Sharon yelled, "come here this minute!"

Cole sauntered in and asked, "What are you so uptight about? Did you have a bad day at work?"

Sharon clenched her fists, ready to read Cole the riot act, when she decided to try another approach. She knew Cole was defiant and masterful at defeating adults who told him what to do or who got angry when he didn't do what they wanted.

Sharon paused for a moment then asked, "Cole, have you read your horoscope today?"

"What are you talking about? You know I don't read the horoscopes."

"Well listen to this," Sharon opened the morning paper and, with a serious face, began reading, "Aries: Today is the day you will feel an irresistible urge to return Sharon's scissors to the kitchen, bring all the dirty dishes and silverware back to be washed, untangle the phone cord so it reaches the table, and put Sharon's hairbrush back in her bathroom."

"You're kidding me, Sharon. Let me see that!" Cole grabbed for the paper.

"You run and take care of those things, and I'll cut it out for you to read later," Sharon teased.

Cole grinned from ear to ear and said, "Sharon, you're weird." A few minutes later he brought a laundry basket filled with dirty dishes into the kitchen, replaced the scissors, and started working on the phone cord.

Sharon gave Cole a big hug and said, "Thanks, guy!"

On another occasion Sharon asked Cole if he would like help with his procrastination.

"Sharon, it's a family trait. All the guys in our family do it. It's in our genes."

"Well, I have an idea about how you could change it if you want to, but I'm not going to tell you unless you beg me."

"Okay, Sharon, I'm begging. Please, please, please, what's your idea?" Cole joked.

"Do you know that most actions have a beginning, middle, and an end? I notice that you are good at beginnings, fair with middles, and lousy with ends. Either you get a business card that says 'Cole Anderson, Procrastinator, No Job Too Small to Put Off' or you try my ABC Happiness Plan."

Cole asked, "What's an ABC Happiness Plan?"

"I can't tell you, but I can show you. Are you ready?" asked Sharon.

Cole knew he was being tricked once again, but Sharon had a way of helping him save face and making things fun, so he decided to go along with her. "Okay, Sharon, I'm ready."

"We'll start with 'A.' Go to your car and bring in all the towels and blankets that belong in the house."

Cole went to his car and returned with his arms loaded. "What next, Sharon?"

"Here comes 'B.' Take all the towels and blankets in your arms and put them in the washer, add soap, and start the machine. Then stand in front of the machine and see if you can guess what 'C' will be."

"I suppose 'C' is that I'm supposed to fold the stuff and put it away," mused Cole.

"Clever boy. I knew you'd catch on to the ABC Happiness Plan. Aren't you feeling happy? I know I am," Sharon said, laughing.

Cole just shook his head and gave Sharon that special look that said adults can be pretty strange.

Sharon could have turned any of these situations into a confrontation had she insisted that Cole was lazy or defiant. She decided that she wanted to live in harmony rather than in a war zone. The more she relied on her humor, the more Cole pitched in without a battle.

## BE SENSITIVE TO THE NEEDS OF THE UNTRAINED WORKER

Sometimes when teens refuse to work, it is for a very different reason than the laziness or defiance parents often assume. If you waited until your child became an adolescent to involve him or her in household chores, your child may not know how to do the jobs and be unwilling to ask for help. Teenagers' defiance can be a cover for embarrassment.

In many cases, when teens can't do something, it's not because they're inept, but because they're untrained or unskilled. It's difficult for adolescents to admit they don't know how to do something. Teens like to appear as if they know everything and adults know little.

If you've forgotten that it takes time and practice to learn a new skill, you may expect your teen to catch on automatically, especially when he or she looks so grown up. Learning how to do the job and finding time for training and practice is critical for teens. You need to let your teens know it's all right to not know something and that it's okay to ask for help. You can encourage your teens by focusing on their effort instead of complaining about things that are done sloppily or forgotten. Notice how the mother in the following story avoided all criticism as she helped her sons become involved in family chores.

Paul, fourteen, and his brother Todd, sixteen, hadn't been expected to do much around the house. Their mother, Joyce, did the majority of the housework. She tried frequently to get the boys involved, but gave up after numerous hassles and confrontations.

Her friend asked her to attend a book study group for parents of teens. After a few weeks of class Joyce realized she'd never really taught the boys how to do the chores. She'd just assumed that, as they got older, they knew how to do the work but just didn't care. Now she was ready to try again.

The next day she said to the boys, "I can't do everything around here. You two don't do anything to help."

Paul said, "I have practice after school and homework every day."

Todd said, "I have my job after school. I don't have time to do things around here. And anyway, housework is woman's work."

Joyce realized that she had more to do than to teach her sons how to help out. First she needed to deal with their stereotyping, something she had inadvertently fostered.

She said, "I can't blame you for thinking that certain jobs can only be done by certain sexes. Your dad and I have fit the stereotype. But it's time you learned that boys can iron, do dishes, and fold clothes, and girls can wash cars, mow lawns, and empty garbage. Women can change the oil and men can cook dinner. I know this comes as a shock to you, but instead of 'men's work' and 'women's work,' there's just 'work that needs to be done.'"

"Mom, if you think I'm going to let you change the oil in my car while I iron your blouses, you're even stranger than I thought you were," Todd said.

"That's not what I'm asking. Anyway, I've already tried changing the oil in my car, and if you'll remember, I had to call AAA to come to my rescue when I accidentally tightened the oil filter instead of loosening it."

Todd, in all his teenage wisdom and altruism, looked at his mom and said, "Aw, don't let that get you down. Everyone does that at least once. You could try again, Mom."

"Let's make a deal, Todd," Joyce said. "If you drive my car up on those ramps for me, I'll iron your shirt for the dance. Of course," she teased, "if you'd like, I'll teach you how to iron it so you don't have to wait for me to do it."

Paul said, "Really, Mom, how will I do all the work around here and get good grades?"

Joyce responded, "I know you both have lots to do. We're all busy, but it's important to me that we learn to work together. I've made a list of the jobs that I'd like help with. Why don't we start with each of you picking one job to do today or tomorrow. We can start slowly. I'm happy to teach you how to do jobs you haven't done before, if you like."

Joyce presented the boys with a list of twenty jobs. She asked each boy to pick one job. Paul said, "I think I can figure out how to scrub the tub," and Todd said, "I'll do the grocery shopping. If I can use the car Thursday, I can go to the store after work." Joyce thanked the boys for their willingness to help and told them that she wanted to set a time to meet and talk about both jobs.

Joyce asked Paul if she could show him what she used for scrubbing the tub and he agreed. She showed Paul the new scrubber she bought for him to use. They talked about what cleaning product would work, how long the job might take, and what it would look like when completed. Paul even practiced on one spot. Joyce asked, "What do you think?" Paul replied, "It looks pretty good." They set a time for the job to be done. She talked to Todd about the shopping list, what store he planned to go to, how much money he'd need, and the car schedule for Thursday.

Todd came home Thursday with the groceries. While putting them away, Joyce noticed that he'd forgotten two items on the list. Instead of pointing out his mistakes, Joyce said, "Thanks for doing the shopping. I feel so relieved. Your help makes a big difference."

"Thanks, Mom," Todd replied as he picked up a few cans and put them in the cabinet. Joyce added the two items to next week's shopping list.

The next afternoon she heard Paul scrubbing away in the bathroom. A little later she heard the front door close and he was gone. She checked the tub and saw cleanser sprinkled everywhere and soapy residue in the tub. When Paul returned, Joyce asked him to go into the bathroom with her. She looked at the tub and asked, "What do you think?"

"It's not so bad. I was in a hurry because my friends were waiting for me."

"Does this look like what we talked about the other day?"

Paul looked down and said, "I guess not."

"Try again. I know you can finish the job," Joyce said as she walked out of the bathroom.

Later Joyce peeked into the bathroom. Paul had cleaned and rinsed the tub, but he left the scrubber on the floor. She walked down the hall and knocked on Paul's door. "I just wanted to say thanks. Your help is really appreciated. Good night." By focusing on progress, Joyce was teaching her sons they could succeed when they helped the family.

## BE CREATIVE AND CHANGE WHAT ISN'T WORKING

Sometimes your teens are uncooperative because they don't want to do things the way they always have. They're ready for a change. If you notice resistance or procrastination for jobs that used to be done without any trouble, sit down with the family and talk about what's going on. Ask if it's time to change jobs. Are the teens resistant because someone has been nagging them? Is it time for a break from schedules? Do family members need to swap jobs? By the time your children are teens, they may have been doing the same jobs for years. Perhaps they picked the jobs when they were much younger and are tired of them or would prefer doing something else.

In one family the teenage daughter had been clearing the table for nine years. Since no one else in the family was complaining about their jobs, she thought she was stuck. Her mother noticed she had to call her daughter four or five times to clear the table, so she asked if there was a problem. Her daughter said she was tired of clearing the table after all these years. Her mother suggested she bring this up at the family meeting so everyone could talk about redistributing the jobs.

"But what if no one else wants to change?" the girl asked.

"Your problems are as important as the other family members'. A family should help one another," said Mother. "We can work this out."

Often routines that worked when children were younger become disrupted by teenagers' work and social obligations. When a thirteen-year-old boy made the cheerleading squad at school, his new schedule interfered with the normal routine. Since practices were held daily from 5:00 p.m. to 6:30 p.m., he could no longer set the table or make the salad for the family's 6:00 p.m. dinner. At a family meeting, he decided he could take out the trash and empty the dishwasher for his sister if she could do his chores until the end of cheerleading season. Adjusting to schedule changes instead of automatically picking up the slack for a busy teen is easiest when your family holds regular family meetings.

When sixteen-year-old Mandy made the volleyball team, she explained that she wouldn't have time to do her chores if she was going to keep up her grades and be on the team. After several weeks of practice, her family was exhausted and irritated by her lack of participation. Her laundry sat in the washing machine for days, monopolizing the laundry room and acquiring that pungent odor of mildew. However, she found plenty of time to talk on the phone with her boyfriend. Her brother David resented doing her chores while she sat with the phone glued to her ear.

Dad asked that the family sit down and talk about a problem that came up. At the meeting, David complained about Mandy's lack of cooperation. When Mandy insisted she didn't have time to help the family, and mentioned that she "washed her dishes, so what was the problem," her father Dennis said, "Mandy, it's unacceptable for you to not help. We are willing to help you find a way to contribute that fits into your schedule, but all of us are busy and have other commitments too, and we're tired of doing your share."

"I have an idea," said David. "You don't have practice or games on Wednesday. If you can't get your work done during the rest of the week, maybe you could do it all Wednesday afternoon before dinner. I bet your boyfriend would even help if you asked him."

"I'm not asking my boyfriend to do chores for our family. He has enough to do at his place. And how am I supposed to do everything in one afternoon?" Mandy complained.

"That's not our problem," said Dennis. "You have all week, and I think David has an excellent idea. I'd like to try it out for the next two weeks. Unless you can think of a better plan, we'll hold dinner on Wednesday until you complete your work."

"I don't think that's fair, but I suppose I don't have a choice," grumbled Mandy.

The first week, Mandy's chores did not get done. On Wednesday, her father went to her room when he got home from work. "Mandy, it's my night to make dinner. Why don't you let me know when you are almost done with your chores so I can start cooking. I'm making spaghetti, and that takes about a half hour."

"I can't believe you're going to stick with that ridiculous idea of David's," said Mandy. "It will take me till midnight to finish everything!"

Dennis said, "I'll put out some snacks for everyone. We'll wait until you're done to have dinner."

Mandy reluctantly started working and completed all her chores within two hours. The family sat down to dinner at nine. Dennis set the table with candles and had the stereo playing. Not a word was said about the late time or Mandy's attitude. The following week Mandy had her work done by seven. At the family meeting, she said the new plan would work just fine during volleyball season. Everyone breathed a sigh of relief.

A willingness to be creative instead of insisting on doing things the same way turned many potential power struggles into workable solutions for everyone. Another way to win cooperation with teens is to work with them to solve problems instead of telling them what they have to do.

## PRACTICE JOINT PROBLEM SOLVING

Conner was a helpful boy who was very involved in family responsibilities. When he turned thirteen and started junior high school, he informed his mother he would no longer clean his room each day or eat breakfast with the family. He thought these things were childish and he was too old to continue the activities he did as a child. Besides, school started earlier, and he didn't want to get up "before the birds" to eat some "stupid breakfast."

Conner's mother, Ginny, did what most parents of adolescents do: she argued, nagged, threatened, and yelled. Naturally, none of those efforts improved the situation. After several months, she realized that Conner was older and ready for a change. She reminded herself that the family was a team, that she was the coach, that when she stepped back and slowed down, she could see Conner's point of view, and that she needed to focus her energy about a change by asking for Conner's help to find a solution. She decided to have the conversation when she wasn't angry to see if they could work out a solution they were both comfortable with. Ginny knew nothing could be accomplished by arguing at the time the problem was occurring and that she and Conner needed to agree on a time to talk. She approached Conner with a request to talk together, and they agreed to meet when he got home from school that afternoon.

"Conner," Ginny began, "I'm tired of fighting with you every morning; I realize I haven't been treating you respectfully. Do you think we could come up with a routine we could both live with? When you don't have breakfast with us, I miss spending time with you. We hardly ever see each other anymore. I also understand that you don't want to clean your room every day, but I'm not comfortable with the room never getting cleaned."

Conner said, "You don't realize that I'm getting older and you still treat me like I'm a little kid. I'm too tired in the morning to get up earlier to have breakfast, and I want to spend time with my friends after school."

"Do you think it would be too much to clean your room once a week?" asked Ginny.

"Of course not. I could do it as part of the cleaning we do on Sunday," Conner suggested.

"That's okay with me as long as you make arrangements to do it later in the day if you spend the night at a friend's."

"No problem, Mom," Conner said. "If you would drive me to school in the morning so I don't have to ride my bike, we could spend time together in the car. I hate riding my bike to school."

"Conner, I could drive you on Mondays, Thursdays, and Fridays, but how would you get home if you don't have your bike?"

Conner said, "That's easy, I could get a ride home with my friends."

"I feel better about us working this out together," said Ginny, "but I'm still concerned about one thing. If you forget to clean your room on Sunday, I would like a plan so that it gets done without me having to remind or nag you."

"If I forget, you could tell me during dinner, and then I'll do it before I watch TV," suggested Conner.

"Wouldn't that be inconvenient for you?" Ginny asked.

"Sure, so maybe that will help me remember better."

Ginny and Conner both felt better. They had a win/win plan with a deadline they both could live with and a system for dealing with forgetfulness. When a teen is part of the problem-solving process, he or she will either do what was agreed without reminders or respond positively to a parent who actively follows through by saying, "What was our agreement?"

## LOOSEN THE REINS AND ENCOURAGE MORE ADULT RESPONSIBILITIES

Sometimes adults underestimate what teenagers can do and overestimate what parents should do. As your teens get older, let them take over more responsibility, such as doing all the laundry or the grocery shopping. Once your teen has a driver's license, let him or her do the carpooling or errands that involve the car to get more driving practice. You can teach your teen how to change the oil or do the tune-ups, or keep a service record and take the car to the garage when maintenance is required.

Many teens enjoy working outside the home at jobs such as babysitting, house-sitting, washing cars, doing yard work, handling paper routes, doing housecleaning, working as computer consultants, working in local stores or restaurants, walking dogs, tutoring younger children, or hiring out for cleanup projects or construction jobs. We suggest you encourage your teen to work part time and continue their allowance without reducing the amount just because they are earning money. (See chapter 9 for more information.) Talk with your teen about the extra costs they can cover with their additional money, or encourage them to save for bigger purchases like cars, college, deposits on apartments, and so on.

In one family, the parents were able to hire their son to set up a computer network and keep the computers in working order at their office. The boy felt important and capable and was also able to provide extra income to cover some of his personal expenses. The family took this opportunity to sit down, reevaluate their plan for household work, and make adjustments in his responsibilities.

Even though your teen may be able to handle more responsibility, he or she may make a mistake by taking on too much. If your teens take on more than they can handle, you can help them improve an out-of-control situation without rescuing them. Phil's family had an opportunity to do this when seventeen-year-old Phil purchased his first car. Phil decided he could save money by buying an old car and restoring it. He told his parents he would do the body and engine work with his friends. His mother was concerned as people didn't work on cars in the neighborhood. Phil said, "No problem, I'll work on the car in the garage."

"But, Phil," said his mother, "that's where I park my car."

Phil's father said, "He can use my side of the garage and I'll park on the street until he's done. How long do you think it will take to fix your car up, son?"

"With all the help my friends will give me, I should have the car done in a month," said Phil, deep in the magical thinking most teenagers excel in. Phil's mother wasn't thrilled with the idea, but she agreed to give it a try.

Soon Phil had his tools and car parts spread everywhere in the garage, and neither parent could park inside. His friends soon lost enthusiasm for the project and so did Phil when he found out how long it took to hand sand a car. The harder the job got, the less time Phil spent working on the car. And since the car was up on blocks, it couldn't be moved.

Mom could see Phil was in over his head, so she chose to discuss the car situation at a family meeting. Mom and Dad discovered that not only was Phil overwhelmed, but the car he was restoring was an embarrassment because nobody in Phil's school drove that type of car. Getting the real issue on the table helped the family devise a plan to get rid of the car. Dad helped Phil put the wheels back on; Mom helped Phil write an ad for the paper; and Phil put the rest of the parts back together. Everyone was relieved when someone bought the car and towed it away.

That left Phil a teenager without a car. Now it was time to help him to figure out how to take on the responsibility of procuring and maintaining an appropriate vehicle. There are many ways to handle this issue. The options range from parents paying for the car and all the expenses to the teen buying the car and paying all the expenses. Whatever the decision, it should be handled in a respectful manner.

Phil's family sat down together and looked at the costs involved in purchasing and owning a car. It was clear that Phil would need financial assistance. His parents agreed to buy him an inexpensive car if Phil paid for insurance, maintenance, and repairs. Phil agreed and found a part-time job to pay for his expenses. The agreement was that Phil could drive the car if the insurance was up-to-date and the car was safely maintained. If he got behind in any of his payments, he would place the car keys on the table and not drive the car until he caught up.

After a couple of months, Phil quit his job because he didn't like working and instead sold one possession after another to pay for the upkeep on his car. When he ran out of things to sell, he told his parents, "Owning a car is too much responsibility. I'd like to sell it and ride my bike."

Instead of rescuing him, Phil's parents wisely agreed. "We'll do our best to share our cars with you. When you are ready to try owning a car again, let us know. We'll put the money we make selling your car in a special account, and you can use that to help purchase your next car. If you would like a nicer car, you can add to the account until you're ready to take the money out for a car." Phil liked that idea and was relieved to have more time for his friends and school. Phil was part of the decision-making process all along, and he thought the agreements were fair.

What was meant to be a solution to the car problem in the Rivera family developed into a bigger problem. They began connecting school grades to the use of the car, a popular method many of their friends used to motivate success in school.

Lucy and Manny Rivera had three children—Maria, eighteen, Carlo, sixteen, and Phillipe, eleven. Maria did well in school, but Carlo's grades were poor. His parents knew how important it was for Carlo to drive, so they came up with a rule that he had to get Bs in order to use the car. They told Carlo, "Get Bs or no keys," thinking this would motivate him to improve his grades. The Riveras also pointed out that they were able to save money on their insurance because of Maria's A- average at the junior college and could get the same discount when Carlo produced a B- average report card.

Carlo promised that he'd work on his grades. In the meantime, he volunteered to do any errand that involved driving so he could use the car more. He began picking up his younger brother, going to the store, putting gas in the car, and picking up his sister from work. Most of his friends were still fifteen, so Carlo felt pretty important when they asked him for rides.

Manny asked Carlo how he was doing in school several times, and each time Carlo assured him things were just fine. When the time came for his quarterly progress report, Lucy asked to see it, but Carlo "forgot" it at school. When Manny and Lucy received Carlo's final grade report and saw his C- average, they were stunned.

When Carlo returned from picking up Phillipe at soccer practice, his father met him at the door. Manny held up the report card and yelled, "This is what you think are fine grades! They're terrible! You're not driving the car until you pull them up."

"You don't care about me," Carlo yelled back as he ran out of the house, slamming the door. Lucy listened to this and realized it was going to be difficult to take over the errands Carlo had been doing. She wasn't happy with the way things had turned out.

Carlo didn't use the car for the next week. Then one afternoon he told his mother he had a report due and asked if he could use the car just to go to the library. Since it was school related, Lucy relented.

"Just to go to the library. What time will you be home? I have to pick Phillipe up at practice."

"I don't know. I should be done by 5:30. I can pick Phillipe up."

Lucy thought for a moment then said, "I guess that's okay."

On the way to the library, Carlo waved at two friends who then motioned him to stop. When they found out he was going to the library, they asked for a ride downtown. Carlo said "Sure," and dropped his friends off at the mall.

When Carlo got home with his brother, his mother glared at him, "You were supposed to go to the library, not go driving around with your friends."

Carlo looked shocked, "What? I did go to the library. I just dropped my friends off at the mall. It was no big deal."

"Well, your father saw you downtown and he's furious. You weren't supposed to be driving anyway."

People in the Rivera household were feeling confused, angry, and hurt. Teens are seldom motivated to improve their grades by threats that they'll lose an unrelated privilege. Not allowing Carlo to drive was actually counterproductive in that it robbed him of the opportunity to cooperate and contribute in his family by running errands.

If the Riveras wanted to relate Carlo's grades to his using the car in a respectful and logical way, they might have had Carlo check the rates at their insurance company. He would have discovered the difference between the regular rates and the good student discount rates. The Riveras could let Carlo know they'd be willing to pay the amount for the good student rate. If it turned out that he didn't qualify, he could make up the difference. That way it would be up to him and respectful to all.

When a teen doesn't see the logic of a plan or thinks an adult is controlling, unreasonable, or unfair, the potential for rebellion, either outward or inward, increases. When teens rebel with passive (inward) power, they appear to be doing what you want, but are actually doing what they want instead. Teens may use excuses like "I forgot," "I lost it," or "I ran out of time" to defy you. When teens decide to do things and the work is meaningful to them, they are capable of great effort.

## TAP INTO TEENAGE HUMANITARIANISM

Teens are very altruistic and concerned about the greater good. Help your teens understand that keeping agreements is a trust issue, and that their behavior impacts others. Knowing they make a difference in the family helps teens act respectfully. Let your teen know that you do not wish to take advantage of him or her, nor do you want to be taken advantage of. By helping your teen understand that being part of a family means respecting each other and not taking relationships for granted, you can motivate your teen to care more about others' needs.

Young people can make great accomplishments when they feel what they are doing is meaningful. Twins Shiloh and Sabrina illustrate this. At age sixteen, the twins disliked routine family chores, but they were more than happy to work together on projects that had long-lasting benefits for the family. One summer they painted the outside of the house. The next year they put in a sprinkler system and planted a garden. When the family wanted to remodel a room but found the cost too great, Shiloh and Sabrina volunteered to do the labor on the project. Their uncle got them started and supervised the work, but the twins did most of the project. The family was thrilled with the new room, taking everyone who came to visit for a look. Visitors were amazed at the professional job done by two eighteen-year-olds and complimented Shiloh and Sabrina profusely. The twins laughed and said, "We'd rather paint ten houses than do dishes every night. Our folks are willing to pick up the slack during the week because they know we can be counted on for the big jobs!"

If you treat your teens with respect and allow for the changes in their behavior that come with adolescence, you can enjoy them more as well as get a lot more done.

# 9

# Raising
# Money-Savvy Kids

Why are we including a chapter on money in a book on chores without wars? You're probably thinking this is the part of the book where we talk about paying kids for doing chores. Actually, we'd like to suggest just the opposite. Although many parents connect allowance with chores, we invite you to change that thinking and separate chores from allowance.

Before you throw your hands up in disbelief or stop reading this chapter altogether, take a few minutes to answer these questions.

- Do you want your kids to learn about setting priorities?
- Do you want them to learn about planning ahead?
- Would you like it if they developed self-discipline?
- Is it important to you that your children learn to defer gratification?

- Do you want your kids to feel a sense of control over the decisions they make?

If you answered yes to any of these questions, we'd like to share a remarkable piece of information with you. Properly used, the allowance is a vehicle that allows your children to acquire all those qualities. And while they're becoming more capable, they learn to be money savvy in the process.

Some of you may think children shouldn't have to worry about money. It's bad enough to have to do so as an adult, right? We've found just the opposite to be true. The more children understand about earning, saving, and managing their money, the less they actually worry about money. The more children know how to deal with money, the less likely they are to solve their money problems through tantrums, begging, stealing, selling drugs to make a killing, or making promises they never keep to pay you back when you bail them out.

It's not possible to avoid teaching your children about money, even if you try. Your children start learning about money early in life. Consider this. When two-year-old Jesse wants a toy at the grocery store and pitches a fit when his mom says no, does he learn that if he screams loud enough to drown out all those words his mom is using, eventually he'll get that toy? If so, he's just learned his first lesson about money. Is it the lesson his mom wants him to learn? Probably not, and worse yet, what will this lesson look like twenty years down the road?

How about when four-year-old Shelly gets angry because you are trying to explain that one quarter is more than three nickels? As you try and try to explain the difference to her and all she does is cry, do you give her the three nickels and keep the quarter for yourself, stifling a giggle till she's out of the room? If so, she just learned a lesson about money. Is it the lesson you'd like her to learn? Is she still confused about the value of money in her thirties, expecting someone else to figure it out for her?

What do you think your three- and seven-year-olds are learning when they hear you and your partner yelling about purchases, bounced checks, credit card balances, or loans to older children? Again, are these the lessons you want to be teaching?

Fast forward to junior high school when your thirteen-year-old won't go to school without name-brand jeans and tennis shoes. You explain that you can't afford to buy those items. Your thirteen-year-old blackmails, manipulates, shames, and wants you to feel guilty until, what? Until you produce the cash for the clothes. Your teen has learned a lesson about money. Is it the lesson you want her to learn? And how about years later when she has your credit card for gas and charges hundreds of dollars to your card without your permission? Or how about when you get her cell phone bill, only to see that she's not only used all the minutes you paid for but about a thousand more? She promises to pay you back, but by then, she has no way to keep that commitment and she's too far in debt to succeed even if she tried. She's also learning lessons about money. But are they the lessons you want her to learn? Better hope that she'll find someone else to take care of her when she overspends as an adult.

Since your children are always making decisions about money it would be better if you could help your children grow up learning how to handle money responsibly by starting them on an allowance immediately. We'd like to help you send your children into the world with the skills they need. Then they can earn money, spend what they have instead of going into debt, pay their bills on time, save for what is important to them, pay back loans, and feel the sense of power that comes from knowing they are on top of their finances.

Parents who lack skills and training in money management often have difficulty deciding how to handle money with their children. Considering that we live at a time when most people struggle with money issues, use too many credit cards, borrow on their houses, and just plain don't know how to manage their money responsibly, odds are that without a plan and skills, you'll have a tough time teaching your children something you don't know. The good news is that even if you have less-than-stellar money management skills, you can overcome your habits and help your children become good money managers by using the suggestions in this chapter, starting with the allowance.

## WHAT IS AN ALLOWANCE AND WHY IS IT IMPORTANT?

Why is there so much confusion about the benefits of the allowance as a training tool? Because you, like other parents, have preconceived notions about how an allowance should work based on either how you grew up or conclusions you've made without testing them out. Instead of thinking that everyone who lives in a family needs to chip in with the chores because they are part of the family and that children need an allowance so they can learn about handling money, here are more common thoughts about allowances:

- Allowances are pay for work.
- If children don't work, they don't get an allowance.
- The threat of taking away an allowance is one of the best ways to keep kids in line.
- Children don't need an allowance because you'd prefer to control and monitor what they spend money on, and you can do that by giving children money when you think it's best.
- Kids have to learn to work for their money, because it's the way of the world. No one gets something for nothing. Chores are the way children learn about "earning a living."

Where did you get these ideas? You developed these attitudes when you were children. Many of you received money from your parents when you were children. Perhaps your parents gave you money as a reward or a bribe for doing chores, for "good" behavior, or for doing something that pleased them. Perhaps your parents withheld money as punishment if you didn't do the chores or misbehaved in some other way. Or perhaps you were given money arbitrarily, in varying amounts depending on your parents' whims. Some of you may have received money for good grades or lost hope of receiving any because of poor grades. Perhaps your family struggled financially just to survive and there was no money for you. Whatever the reason, if you agree with those common beliefs, you might be cutting off your nose to spite your face, along with your children's noses at the same time. Your children need money so they can learn how to plan, make choices, set priorities, and realize the power that comes with managing money well. To do so, you need to give them money in the form of an allowance. We suggest that you start early, like Kay did, in the following story.

Kay had her shopping list in hand as she entered the supermarket with her toddler, Susie. As she lifted her three-year-old daughter into the shopping-cart seat, Susie lunged forward trying to reach the candy and toy machines close by. "I want candy," Susie cried, expressing her first need for money. Kay said no, and Susie screamed all the way through the checkout line until she got to the car.

Parents might think suggesting that a child this age can understand or handle an allowance is silly. We believe that young children understand far more than adults give them credit for and that before they are five, they begin making decisions about themselves and their world that they carry into adulthood. You have a wonderful opportunity to begin training your children to handle money by allowing them to make small mistakes and learn from those mistakes.

When Kay returned home, she sat on the floor with her daughter and said, "Susie, you wanted something at the store. I think you're ready for an allowance so you can get the things you want the next time we go there. Would you like that?" Susie smiled at her mother. Kay said "Good! Friday will be payday. I'll give you a quarter for candy." Susie started playing with her blocks again.

Friday, Kay gave Susie a quarter and said, "Here is your allowance, sweetie." Susie took the quarter, looked at it, and put it in her pocket. Two days later Kay found the pants with the quarter still in Susie's pocket. She did not say anything to Susie, nor did she return the quarter.

On the next trip to the supermarket, Susie ran to the candy counter and said, "I want candy!"

Kay asked, "Have you brought your allowance?" Susie looked up at her and repeated, "I want candy," and started to cry.

Kay replied calmly, "Next time bring your allowance and you can get some." Instead of feeling sorry for Susie or rescuing her, she gently took Susie's hand, walked her over to the cart, and lifted her into the seat. Kay knew that her daughter could learn from a small disappointment and that the lessons would only get harder if she didn't have the courage to follow through while Susie was little.

During the next few months Susie often lost her quarter, but sometimes she remembered to bring it in her little change purse and was able to make her purchase. Gradually she learned that she had to remember her allowance if she wanted to buy something at the store, and she did.

If your child is older and isn't getting an allowance yet, it's never too late to start. Read on. The ideas in the rest of the chapter will help you get started with older children.

## HOW MUCH ALLOWANCE DO I START WITH?

The amount of an allowance should be based on five factors: your *child's age, your child's needs and wants, your child's experience with money, the family resources*, and *your discretion*. It is not based on what your child's friends are getting. Twenty-five cents a week was appropriate for Susie at age three. She couldn't buy much for a penny or a nickel. As a rule of thumb, you might figure on twenty-five cents for a three-year-old and increase the amount by twenty-five cents for each year the child has had experience with money. When this formula stops working, it is time to negotiate again. The best place to do this is at the family meeting (see chapter 7).

## HELPING YOUR CHILDREN LEARN HOW TO CREATE A MONEY PLAN

To help older children learn to figure out how much money they need and how to live within their means, you can introduce the idea of creating a money plan. This works well with school-age children, beginning in elementary school and continuing through college. When your child learns to manage money during the school years, he or she is building skills to carry into adulthood.

A good way to begin helping your child learn to plan is to ask, "What are your expenses?" Many children respond by saying, "I don't know." If this happens, ask your children what items they want you to buy for them during the week, and say, "Let's make a list." Be sure to include the items and the amount needed for each item for a week. You might remind them of purchases you remember them asking for. The goal is to start your children thinking ahead about what they need and want and begin calculating those costs.

Children don't have to think about what they buy or how much things cost when someone else pays. That practice encourages "unconscious" spending. When they are out shopping and see something they want, they simply ask you to buy it. Your child doesn't have to put that purchase in a context of whether he or she has the money for it or not. Whether you buy it or not often depends more on your whims than on your actual financial situation. We have often heard a child ask for something and the parent respond, "I don't have enough money." The child replies, "Write a check" or "Go to the ATM." Patterns of uninformed, irresponsible, or unconscious spending developed in childhood often continue in adulthood.

The parents of a seven-year-old, a twelve-year-old, and a seventeen-year-old decided to give the kids an allowance. They said, "We have been paying for the things you ask for during the week. Sometimes you want something and we say no and you get angry. Sometimes we feel irritated that you are asking for money. We realize that you need money and would like to help you learn more about managing money by having some of your own each week. We would like to start you each with an allowance, and we need to know what you think you will need each week." After an initial "I don't know," the children each made a list with the following items.

## SAMPLE MONEY PLAN

| Seven-year old | | Twelve-year-old | | Seventeen-year-old | |
|---|---|---|---|---|---|
| Gum | $ .60 | Movie | $12.00 | Movie | $5.00 |
| Book | $2.00 | Gum | $ .60 | Gas | $10.00 |
| | | Snacks | $8.00 | Snacks | $10.00 |
| | | Hot lunches | $3.00 | Makeup | $3.00 |
| | | | | Cell phone | $10.00 |
| | $2.60 | | $23.60 | | $55.00 |

Once the kids have listed the items and the amounts, you have identified your child's *needs* and *wants*. Needs are the essentials, the things to be taken care of first, while wants are the extras, the things that make life fun. Neither is negotiable, but that doesn't mean that you have to provide the entire amount desired. Next, you consider what might be appropriate for children of that *age, what things really cost, what is necessary* (since your children have little experience with money at this point, you need to help with what things cost and what is necessary until they acquire some experience), and what the *family resources* are. Then, as the parents, use *your discretion* and decide the amount of money you are willing to provide.

Once you have agreed on an amount for the allowance, give your child his or her money and set up a time to reevaluate the amount. We suggest waiting at least a week but no more than a month to reevaluate. In the meantime, leave it up to your child to decide how to spend his or her money. That's how your child gathers experience. Your child will soon learn that if she wants to buy books but spends the money going to a movie, there won't be enough for the books. Decide ahead of time how much money you are willing to give up control over so your children can learn from their mistakes (and they *will* make some).

Starting out a seventeen-year-old with $55 a week may be more than you can comfortably give up control of and more than she needs to gain experience in handling money. Or, if your child wants to spend $10 a week on snacks, you may be unwilling to let him spend that much money in that way. The parents in the example above felt the seven-year-old's request for $2.60 was reasonable, so they agreed on that amount. The twelve-year-old's request was too high, so the parents said they felt $10.00 a week was more appropriate. They suggested the child might save some of his allowance each week and go to a movie once a month, or chip in with a sibling or friends to rent a movie. They reminded their young teen that they had ideas for work or extra jobs for pay (see more information on jobs for pay in this chapter) to help him make up the deficit.

The seventeen-year-old's request exceeded the parents' estimate by $15.00 a week. The parents explained their own financial limits to her and said they would be happy to do some problem solving to help her figure out how she could make things work. Instead of denying her expenses, the parents were willing to help her take the responsibility to find a solution. When she agreed to their help, they again mentioned the movie rental idea or going to the movies less often. They also suggested several ideas for part-time work. They offered to take her to the local discount food store to cut the cost of snacks by buying in bulk. They suggested she ask her friends to chip in a dollar for gas to help cover the cost of picking them up and taking them to school.

Their teenage daughter asked if she could earn extra money when she babysat for her seven-year-old sister. Her parents considered this request and said they would be willing to pay her on weekends, but not during the week. She thanked them for being willing to help her earn extra money. The family agreed to try out the new allowance plan for a month and evaluate it at a family meeting.

Once the amount of the allowance is agreed upon, it should be given on a regularly scheduled day and time. After some discussion, the above family decided Friday at 6:30 would be *payday*. Parents are responsible for remembering to provide the allowance at the agreed-upon time, and for being consistent and reliable. Keep your agreement. Don't make your children have to nag or beg for the money you said would be theirs.

## INTRODUCE THE BIG PICTURE TO YOUR CHILDREN

When teaching children how to be money savvy, it's important to help them understand the concept of the big picture. Begin by explaining about cash flow, the relationship between the money coming in (income) and the money going out (expenses). How your child manages cash flow will have a direct impact on his or her financial health.

To help your children have an accurate picture of their current situation, have them list all their sources of income: allowance, work (part-time job, jobs for pay), gifts, and from any other sources. Then have them list all of their expenses (needs and wants). Finally, calculate the totals. It's crucial to set things up so they have enough income to cover their expenses or, even better, to have a surplus (more income than expenses).

Most people do okay managing their regular (weekly or monthly) expenses. In the beginning, start your young child with an allowance that involves a few expenses that occur weekly. We call this a *simple* allowance. Your child gets an allowance (income) once a week to spend on needs and wants for that week.

As your children get older, gradually increase their level of responsibility and planning by moving to an *expanded* allowance. Here, not every expense is a regular weekly expense, so you introduce the concept of putting money away in *reserve* for nonregular expenses and "rainy day" expenses due in the short term. Some of these expenses may occur only once a month or just a few times a year. Suggest your children reserve designated funds in an envelope, piggy bank, or a jar so they will be available when the expense comes due. At that time, your children can take out the money and spend it on the designated item. It is important to account for those expenses and calendar them when helping your children set up their money plans. Warn your children about the temptation to take money out of reserve for a different purpose while assuring themselves they will replace the amount in time before it comes due. Also, teach your children that reserves are different from *savings*, which is money that is put away for long-term goals (education, car purchase, apartment deposit, college). These funds are best placed in a bank with deposits made regularly.

As your children get older and gain more experience managing money responsibly, you can move them to a *complete* allowance. This is the point where they are managing all their money, income and expenses.

The Harrises wanted to teach their son, Ben, to be responsible with money. They stared training him with a *simple* allowance at a young age. By the time Ben was five and started kindergarten, he had his wallet that he kept in his pocket whenever he thought he might need to have money with him. Together he and his parents decided he was responsible enough to handle his money for milk and added this to his list of weekly expenses. Each Monday Ben brought his wallet to school and proudly gave his teacher his milk money for the week. When Ben told his parents he wanted to buy a car when he got older, they took him to the local bank and opened an account for savings and included that expense in his money plan. He began making regular deposits to his savings account every month.

Each year before the start of the new school year, Ben and his parents revised his money plan for the coming year. They gradually increased the amount of his allowance along with the items on his expense list as his needs and wants changed, which gave him more practice in his increasing skills of money management. They saw Ben handling money responsibly and by the time he was ten, Ben had been managing his *expanded* allowance with several envelopes in his drawer where he kept his money in *reserve*.

One day he asked his mother if he could go to the mall and get a video with a friend and when she said he could, he surprised her by asking for money. She suggested he check his envelope for videos. Ben said he had used that money at the movies last week. Mrs. Harris looked at him and smiled, and Ben called his friend back and said he'd like go to the mall next month. Instead of yelling or lecturing, she was allowing Ben to experience the consequences of his spending decisions and learning from them.

By the time Ben was sixteen, he had income from a part-time job in addition to his allowance and he was managing the majority of his financial affairs. He no longer used envelopes, he had opened a second bank account for his *reserve* account, and he was using a debit card to handle his nonregular expenses. This gave him practice using "plastic" in a responsible way. His mother helped him learn to use a checking account and also gave him a mall credit card (with an agreed-upon limit) to make his clothing purchases. Ben would be leaving for college in another year and a half, and both he and his parents were feeling confident that Ben was ready to manage a *complete* allowance where he would be financially responsible and live within his means when he was away. He was definitely money savvy.

Here's a tip for handling those expenses that occur at different times throughout the year. Help your children plan for these expenses, which utilize their *reserve* funds, by creating a calendar for these expenses, like the one below.

| Month | Expenses | Amount |
|-------|----------|--------|
| January | Molly's birthday, oil change, haircut | |
| February | Valentine's Day gift | |
| March | Car registration | |
| April | Haircut, Mom's birthday | |
| May | Mother's Day, summer clothes | |
| June | Father's Day, insurance | |
| July | Haircut, oil change, pool dues | |
| August | ======== | |
| September | School clothes and supplies, Dad's birthday | |
| October | Halloween party, Parents' anniversary | |
| November | Concert, haircut | |
| December | Christmas gifts, insurance, ski trip | |

## SUPPLEMENTS TO AN ALLOWANCE— JOBS FOR PAY

As we mentioned at the beginning of the chapter, we don't suggest paying family members to do regular household work. We agree with Rudolf Dreikurs, who said, "There should be no connection at all between chores and allowance. Children do chores because they contribute to the family welfare. They get allowance because they share the benefits" (Dreikurs and Soltz 1964). Household jobs, which need to be done so the household can function, should be kept separate from allowances. A danger in paying kids for doing these jobs is that it cheapens their efforts and they may learn to do work only when they get something for it. Will they pick up their socks only when they get five cents a sock or wash the dishes if they get a dollar? Being a member of a family means sharing the responsibility for work to be done.

We do, however, suggest paying the children for jobs that we would hire someone to do. For instance, one father was taking his car to the local car wash, spending $8 each time. When his kids asked for ways to make extra money, he told them he'd be happy to hire them to do the job for the same amount of money. We recommend keeping a list of jobs for pay along with the amount to be paid for each job on a bulletin board or on the refrigerator so anyone who wants to earn extra money can do so. We suggest discussing standards and working out how payment will be made before the work begins and paying *after* the job is completed. This can prevent arguments about unfinished or sloppy work. Here is a list of jobs for pay that a family made for their children.

### JOBS FOR PAY

| | |
|---|---|
| Wash windows | $1.00 (inside and out) |
| Clean counters | $ .50 |
| Give the dog a bath | $3.00 |
| Wash the car | $8.00 |
| Stack wood | $5.00 an hour |

Ten-year-old Gloria and her eight-year-old brother Dirk were home on a Saturday afternoon. Gloria decided she wanted to buy a new book. She looked in her wallet and realized she was short about three dollars. Payday was Sunday and her parents didn't make advances. She remembered the list of "Jobs for Pay" that her family compiled together. She went to the refrigerator and saw that her parents would pay $8 to have the family car washed. When she asked her mother to back the car into the driveway so she could wash it, Dirk heard her and chimed in, "I want to wash the car, too." Gloria thought for a moment and replied, "Okay, you can help me and we can each get $4."

Mother backed the car into the driveway while Gloria and Dirk got the bucket, hose, soap, rags, and sponges ready. They hosed the car and started washing it. After about a half an hour, Dirk put his sponge down and went into the house to find his mother. "I want my $4. I'm finished. I don't want to do any more." Mother replied, "I pay when the job is done. You'll have to work it out with your sister." Dirk went off to play in the backyard.

An hour later Gloria came to Mother and announced that she was finished and wanted to be paid. She asked if Mother would take her to the bookstore. When Mother went to get her purse, Dirk came in for his half of the money.

Gloria said, "That's not fair. You didn't finish the job, Dirk. You left and went to play while I washed the car. You shouldn't get anything."

Dirk protested, "I did too wash the car, but I got tired."

"Well I don't think half the money is fair. You didn't do half the work," Gloria cried.

Mother returned with the money and said, "Dirk did some of the work, but he didn't finish. What would feel fair to you, Gloria?"

"Well, he shouldn't get half. How about if I get $6 and Dirk gets $2?"

"I want more. I washed the tires and they're hard to do. That's why I got tired," cried Dirk.

"How will you work this out?" Mother asked.

"How about $3 for Dirk and $5 for me," Gloria responded. That was something they all could agree on. Mother distributed the money, then took Gloria to get her book.

## SHOULD WE INTERFERE WITH OUR CHILDREN'S SPENDING?

It is important that your children have freedom of choice in their spending. You may worry that they will make a spending mistake. They will, and that's how they'll learn. You might think an item is overpriced or of poor quality. Motivated by your fear of mistakes, you tell your child it is not okay to buy the item in question. You give your rationale, but your child probably won't see it the same way that you do. In fact, he or she may feel thwarted and think you are unfair and perceive your behavior as an effort to control. After all, whose allowance is it? In an effort to protect your children, you rob them of an opportunity to learn by experiencing the consequences of their behavior (a wonderful teacher for us all), create resentment, and damage your relationship. Hardly the results you intended!

The following actions will help you to have influence with your children and help them to learn good decision-making skills:

1. Follow the *One Comment Rule*. That means you share your opinions one time only, without insisting your child follow them.
2. Support your child by being nonjudgmental.
3. Acknowledge your child's feelings.
4. Allow your child to experience the consequences of his or her spending decisions.
5. Talk with and help your child assess what he or she has learned from the experience.

Twelve-year-old Maria and her mother, Celeste, were shopping for tennis shoes. When Maria found the pair she'd been looking for, Celeste gasped at the $105 price tag. She'd never spent that much for tennis shoes for herself! Secretly she hoped they wouldn't have Maria's size in stock, but the sales clerk returned with a smile and a box of shoes the right size. Maria tried them on and loved them. She looked at her mother who said, "Maria, honey, the budget is tight this month and I can't spend this much on tennis shoes. I expected to spend more like $50. Spending over a hundred dollars is a lot of money for tennis shoes!"

Maria replied, "I know, but everyone has these. I just got money for my birthday. What if you pay the $50 you planned on and I make up the difference with my money? The clerk said I get 10 percent off, which makes them $95. I checked some other stores last week and they were charging $120 to $125 for the same shoes. This is a good price for these, and I really want them."

Celeste refrained from imposing her judgments on her daughter. She listened to her daughter and realized Maria had done some comparison shopping. Celeste was honest about her finances and shared her opinion with Maria instead of imposing it on her. Our experience has been that the more we are honest and share our ideas with our children while letting them experience the consequences of their decisions, the better they get at making wise spending decisions.

Timmy was six and he loved trucks. One day he came home and proudly showed his mother his purchase. He had bought his friend Mark's old truck with his allowance. Mother noticed that the wheels seemed loose and was concerned that Mark had taken advantage of her son, but she didn't say anything. A little while later Timmy came to her crying. "What's wrong?" she asked.

He held up the wheels that had fallen off the truck. "Look what happened," he sniffled. "I'm never buying Mark's toys again!"

"Sounds like you learned something important," his mother replied.

A few days later Timmy told his mother that Mark wanted to sell him another truck and he told Mark he wasn't buying his old toys because they broke. He decided to save his money to buy a new toy truck.

Timmy's mother allowed him to experience the consequences of purchasing an old item and learn from his mistake. She also supported her son by being nonjudgmental, validating his feelings, and helping him understand what he could learn from the experience. This paved the way for future opportunities for Timmy to trust his judgments.

Parents can help their children learn to make wise money decisions by suggesting that the child ask him or herself the following questions prior to making a purchase:

- Do I really need it or do I just want it?
- How useful will it be or is it just another thing to have?

- Can I afford it or would purchasing it later make more sense?
- How much will upkeep and repairs be?
- How long will I use it after I buy it?
- Would something that costs less serve the purpose?
- Do I have the money and will I be paying with cash, check, or credit card?

The answers to these questions can have a profound impact on your child's spending decisions.

## SHOULD YOU GIVE CREDIT OR LOANS?

We do not recommend making loans or extending credit to your children when you begin giving them an allowance. There is a good reason for this. When you are training children in money management, you must think carefully about what you want to teach them. If your goal is to teach them to have their money with them, to think about their decisions, and to use money responsibly, you may end up defeating your purpose by giving loans, especially as a bailout. Hold firm and follow through, even though doing so may be difficult.

Tammy had been giving her son George, age eleven, an allowance for five years. One Saturday George asked if he could go to the movies with his friend Tony. Tammy thought about her plans for the day and replied, "Sure, I can drop you both off downtown this afternoon. What time is your movie?" George said he'd look in the paper. He soon returned and told Tammy the movie started at one o'clock and that he'd need money.

Tammy said, "You got your allowance for this week." George explained that there was a great sale on comic books and he had spent it all on that. Tammy simply replied, "I don't do loans and Tuesday is payday." George nodded and walked away to call his friend. A little while later Tammy noticed Tony had come over and the boys went out to play. That evening George told Tammy that he and Tony would go to the movies next week. Tammy said, "Let me know what time so we can coordinate a ride."

Once good habits of responsible spending are developed, you can lend money to your child when the need arises. For example, your daughter might see a CD she wants at the music store and ask if you'd lend her enough to buy it. She promises to pay you back at home with money from her music envelope. You take a risk (small at first) and make the loan. When you get home your daughter dashes into her room and returns with the money she owes you. She's just established herself as a good credit risk.

If, on the other hand, your daughter dashes to her room to play her CD and later that evening you have to remind her that she owes you money only to get put off again, she has established herself as a poor risk at this time. Refrain from further loans until this one is resolved and explain why. This affords everyone an opportunity to learn from mistakes.

## ADDING MORE FINANCIAL RESPONSIBILITY: THE CLOTHING ALLOWANCE

A clothing allowance is another tool you can use to teach your children lifelong habits of responsible spending. We recommend starting this after your children have had experience with a simple allowance. If you talk about purchases and costs when your children are young, you can start them on a clothing allowance as early as third grade (about eight years of age). By then they are usually ready for another step in handling money. Once again, start the training process with small steps. Eventually you can turn the entire responsibility over to your children (as part of the complete allowance) and let them handle all their clothing purchases.

How much do you spend on your children's clothing each year? Most parents answer, "A lot, but I don't really know the exact amount. I buy what they need." Clothing for children can be very expensive, often putting additional strain on the family finances, and shopping for it can be stressful as well. As your children get older, they become interested in more than whether their clothing fits. The style and brand name can seem crucial to them. Conflicts often develop over what you believe is important and what your children consider important.

If you haven't been paying attention to what you spend on your children's clothing, we suggest you begin to keep track. This will help with future planning. Look through your checkbook and credit card statements for the past few months or collect clothing receipts over the next few months to get an idea. Determine how much money you can or want to make available for your children's clothing in the future. Let your children know this. Establishing clear limits is important in the training process, even though the numbers might not mean much to your children in the beginning.

Children enjoy starting off the school year and heading into summer with new clothes. You can incorporate this into your planning by scheduling clothes buying outings in early fall and in the spring.

Mrs. Thomas had been giving her children an allowance for a few years. Her daughter Dawn turned eight in July and was about to start third grade. Mrs. Thomas decided Dawn was ready to learn more about money and spending and spoke to her husband about what she wanted to do. "I think Dawn is ready to learn more about spending. She already does a good job of managing her allowance, so I'd like to start her on a clothing allowance. I've been keeping track of what we spend on her clothing. I think $600 would work for this year. She can spend up to $300 next month and $300 in the spring. What do you think?"

"Wow, that sounds like a lot of money," he replied.

"It is, but we actually spent a little more than that this past year without really being aware of it. I think this will help us spend less and help Dawn learn more about making spending decisions. I'd like to keep her equipment for soccer separate from this. I don't want her to find she's spent all her clothing allowance and doesn't have money for her uniform. Since it's important to us that she play soccer, I'd like to set it up so she can play without us having to rescue her." Mr. Thomas said, "Good idea. I think I'll like knowing what we're spending instead of waiting to see the bills come in. Maybe we can set aside the money in advance."

The next day the Thomases talked to their daughter about her clothing allowance and made a date to go shopping. Mr. Thomas said he'd like to take his wife and daughter for lunch and shop with them to see how this worked. Mrs. Thomas spent the next half hour showing Dawn, by using paper dolls, how she could make nine different-looking outfits out of three tops and three bottoms.

Later Mrs. Thomas made arrangements to send their son to the sitter's on shopping day, knowing he wouldn't enjoy the shopping trip for his sister.

The following Saturday, the Thomases went to the mall. Dawn brought her calculator with her. In the first store she picked out an armful of clothes and she and her mother went into the dressing room. Dawn tried on everything, discarded some of the items, and added up what was left. The total came to $250. Dawn asked, "What do you think, Mother? I love this sweater and pants outfit."

"I think they're really nice. You have a great eye for color. Do you think you need five new sweaters?" Dawn thought for a minute and said, "Probably not. What I really need is new pants. The ones from last year are too short. I think I'll get the pants outfit and the blue sweater here since it's on sale and go to another store to look more."

"Why don't you model the pants outfit for Dad and tell him your plan?" suggested Mrs. Thomas.

Dawn put on the outfit one more time and went to show her father. "Honey," he said, "you are a great shopper. How about we break for lunch and then continue?"

After lunch, the Thomases continued the process—considering, modeling, adding, subtracting, comparing, wondering, and deciding.

When the family left the mall, Dawn had purchased two sweaters, a jacket, five pairs of pants, socks, underwear, two skirts, a pair of shoes, three pairs of boxers, four pairs of tights, and a dress. Dawn learned a little more about how the marketplace works when the Thomases looked in a discount store and found the pantsuit she had wanted. She bought the outfit at considerably less cost and still had $9.50 remaining in her clothing allowance. She was quite satisfied with herself and asked her parents if she could keep the money she had left over in case she thought of something she wanted later.

Mrs. Thomas said, "I'll make a note in my checkbook that you have $9.50 left, and when you need something, we'll shop again." The Thomases knew that at first it was best to keep a tally of Dawn's spending and pay for the clothing rather than give her the cash. As she gained more experience shopping, they could give her the cash, a mall debit card, or give her money each month to set aside in reserve for clothing. Many children manage a monthly clothing allowance, setting aside money in reserve for big purchases and buying clothes as needed. (A special thank you to Barbara Mendenhall of Petaluma, California, for sharing the clothing allowance commentary.)

As you can see, by following the suggestions in this chapter, children can acquire many of the money management skills that are helpful in life. By the time your children head for college or move out of the house, you will want the training process to be completed, with them assuming full financial responsibility for themselves. We don't mean your children have to be self-supporting, even though many are when they leave home. What we do mean is that, even if your children have their own checking accounts and credit cards, they are responsible for managing and reconciling their accounts. They are making their own spending decisions and are responsible for paying their bills, and they are living within their means.

## CONTINUING THE ALLOWANCE
## THROUGH COLLEGE

If your children do go on to college, you will have to decide how you will be involved financially. Some families cover all the expenses of their college student—room, board, tuition, supplies, books, and living expenses—and some cover nothing. Most are somewhere in between. What works best is for you and your student to decide together what makes sense for your family situation. If you decide to be involved financially, determine how. If your child has had experience managing money successfully, you may be ready to turn all the finances over to him or her. If you haven't done so already, set up a checking account and a credit card so your son or daughter can manage all income and expenses. You may find that many colleges send tuition and housing bills directly to the students. Some don't even send bills! Students need to be responsible for knowing when a payment is due and paying it on time. If it's not made, they can't register for classes, a direct and meaningful consequence for their behavior! You can make deposits into your student's account for tuition and housing costs each month, semester, or quarter, based on the plan both you and your child discuss and agree upon. Deposits for monthly expenses can be handled in the same way. We recommend regular check-ins with your new college student to make needed adjustments and prevent problems from developing.

Mr. and Mrs. Peters had been paying Jordan's tuition and housing expenses plus supplying a monthly allowance of $250. This agreement worked for a year and a half. Every couple of months his parents would ask how things were working, and he would assure them that things were fine. Then, Jordan told his parents he needed a car to drive to a job site for a special project in one of his classes. Since Mr. and Mrs. Peters did not want to buy a car for Jordan, they suggested he ask his grandparents if he could borrow their extra car for the semester. They were happy to help him out.

A few months after Jordan got the car, he called his dad to say he was having trouble meeting expenses. Jordan found that he was spending more money on gasoline than he had anticipated. Mr. Peters told him he would speak with Jordan's mother and get back to him in a day or so. He thanked his son for calling and assured him they would work this out.

Mr. and Mrs. Peters discussed the problem (since it's important that both parents are part of a decision to change an agreement). Already feeling the pinch of increased college costs in their finances, they decided they could help Jordan out with an increase of $50 a month for the next three months, then return to the original $250. They would suggest Jordan look for part-time work to supplement what they were able to provide if he needed more money. They called Jordan that evening to tell him what they were able to come up with.

Jordan was grateful for their help and told them he had already done some checking. He had a possible job lined up for the summer that he hoped might become part time when he started his next semester. In the meantime, the additional $50 would help him meet his obligations. Mr. and Mrs. Peters were grateful that years of spending and planning practice helped Jordan get to this point.

In contrast is the story of Mr. Lyman and his son, Andrew. When Andrew started college, it was the first time he had any responsibility for managing money. His father gave him a credit card and opened a checking account in Andrew's name at the local branch bank. He told Andrew to keep his expenses down to the basics, and Andrew agreed.

Two months after Andrew started school, his father received a call from the bank saying Andrew was overdrawn by $300. Just a few days before, Mr. Lyman noticed that Andrew had restaurant meal charges and expensive clothes on his credit card statement. Furious, he called Andrew to tell him he was overspending and that if he couldn't be more responsible, he would take away the credit card. Andrew begged his father for another chance. He said that things cost much more than he realized, but it was important for him to keep up with his fraternity brothers so he wouldn't get a reputation of being "cheap."

Mr. Lyman was still angry, but he didn't want his son to be unpopular with his fraternity brothers, so he said, "Okay, Andrew, I'll pay these bills and cover the overdraft this time, but don't let it happen again."

"Thanks a lot, Dad. You sure are a great father. I'm glad you understand how tough it is when you're just starting out. I know I learned a lot from this so I'm sure I'll be more careful."

We won't go on with this story, because we're sure you can guess what happens from here.

## HELPING CHILDREN WHO DON'T GO TO COLLEGE

What happens if your children don't go to college and are finished with high school? Once again, financial help at this point may vary from nothing at all to covering all costs. That decision is based on the family's financial situation and your child's circumstances. If your child is trying to support himself, you may want to supplement him financially while he makes the transition from home to independent living. Some parents refuse to help children financially unless they go on to college, but for some young people, college right after high school, or ever, is not the right choice.

We recommend offering support in a respectful way: sit down with your child and find out what his or her plans are. Be extremely clear and specific about how you intend to help. You might offer free rent at your house while your son or daughter gets established in a job or training program. If you are unable to give financial support, you can lend emotional support and ideas, knowing you have valuable lessons to offer.

Many young people feel overwhelmed with the responsibilities after leaving home and are often afraid they won't be able to find a job. They often take advantage of parents who don't set clear and reasonable deadlines.

When Jack finished high school, he told his family he would attend summer school at the junior college to take "How to Study" classes before signing up for college in the fall. He thought he could handle a part-time job along with his course work. The plan sounded good, but Jack slept until noon each day and made no attempt to find a job. He missed the deadline to register for summer school, so the course work never materialized.

Jack said he didn't realize how sick of school he was, and that a summer vacation was just what he needed to be fresh for school in the fall.

His parents said, "Jack, we can see that making the transition from high school to college or the real world is difficult for you. We're willing to help you by providing room and board as long as you are helping yourself. You have until October to get it together. That should give you ample time to find a job, get registered at the junior college, and decide whether taking courses is for you. If you don't want to go to college, we will support your decision, but you can't continue to live here unless you are making progress in taking responsibility for yourself."

Jack said, "That's more than fair. Don't worry, I'll handle it."

When the end of October came, Jack was still unemployed and had decided he didn't want to go to college. It was clear to his parents what help he needed, and they knew it was going to be painful for everyone. They knew Jack was a capable, wonderful person who was scared and confused about how to take the next step. He resisted their attempts to help or give advice, and they respected his right to learn from his experiences. With this in mind, they told Jack it was time to move out. They said they loved him enough to provide him with a growth opportunity. Jack said he understood, packed his bags, and moved in with his friend's family.

It took another six months for Jack to get serious and realize that he didn't want to spend his life sleeping on his friend's bedroom floor and sneaking into his parents' house for showers while they were at work. His parents maintained contact and invited Jack for dinner once a week, which he graciously refused. Jack was angry, but he used his anger to get his life working. He found a job and a house to share. Each step he took to get his life working gave him confidence and pride. A year later, Jack came for dinner and thanked his parents for their faith in him and their help. He said that a lot of his friends were still living with their parents, not working, and not going to school. He knew he would have been in the same place without the "encouragement" from his family.

The earlier you begin helping your children learn money management skills, the easier it is for them when they move away from home. Jack had little responsibility handling money before he left home, so he had some hard lessons to learn without the opportunity to learn gradually and make small mistakes along the way. By starting your children with an allowance, creating jobs for pay, and teaching them to manage a clothing allowance, you give them the skills that make transition into adulthood easier.

## SOME COMMON MISTAKES TO AVOID

Since the concept of giving an allowance without connecting it to chores is such a novel experience for so many of you, we'd like to review some common mistakes that parents make. When you make these mistakes, you are giving with one hand and taking away with the other, undoing all of your hard work to raise money-savvy kids. Consider this a review, as you've already read about all of these mistakes in the chapter.

Mistake #1. You withhold money to punish your child.

- Try again: Once you have committed to give your child an allowance, you are obliged to provide it.

Mistake # 2. You use money as a bribe for good behavior or good grades.

- Try again: Using money as a bribe or reward corrupts the idea that school is for learning and takes away your child's control over money. In the spirit of fun, however, you can make a bet with some children that will motivate them to work harder. You could say, "I'll bet you $50 that you can't raise your grade point average without a tutor. If you win, you get $50. If I win, you get a tutor."

Mistake #3. You tell your child how disappointed you are because he or she made a mistake in a spending decision.

- Try again: Have faith in your child to learn from mistakes, which is possible when you don't complicate things by adding shame and blame.

Mistake #4. You model poor financial management skills, making it harder for your child to be responsible and savvy.

- Try again: Clean up your act and follow the suggestions for a money plan. They work for any age group.

Mistake #5. You attempt to restrict or interfere with your child's spending decisions.

- Try again: Remember the *One Comment Rule* and share your opinions one time only, without insisting your child follow them.

Mistake #6. You forget that allowance and chores aren't connected and you start paying for chores.

- Try again: Remind yourself that chores are something everyone does who lives in the house and allowance is a means that you use for helping your children learn about money.

Mistake #7. You forget or don't follow through with payday, often resulting in arguments about what is due weeks later.

- Try again: If you want your child to be responsible, let it start with you. Make sure you have cash on hand for payday, and if you don't, go get some.

Mistake #8. You rescue or bail out "just this one time" or many times.

- Try again: We know it's tempting, but your children can handle learning from mistakes if you let them. They are building their finance-savvy muscles. When you rescue them, you're weakening the process. The more you rescue, the bigger the mistakes your children are apt to make and the harder it is to let them learn from experience. If you aren't careful, you can undo all your efforts, ending up with a child who thinks it's your job to take care of him or her financially—forever!

# 10

# TEAMWORK IN STEPFAMILIES AND SINGLE-PARENT HOMES

If you are a parent dealing with the aftereffects of divorce, you've probably asked yourself many of the following questions. If you have, you're in good company, because they are typical problems that crop up in stepfamily situations and single-parent homes. Happily, we'd like to assure you that there are solutions for dealing with them, tricks you can teach your children who live in multiple homes, and help for parents who don't have any other adult help or relief. Here are the questions:

- What do I do when a child says "This isn't my family, so I don't have to do chores here" or "I didn't make the mess, so why do I have to clean it?"

- How do I deal with my spouse's children if they won't listen to me?
- How do I stop my partner from treating my children disrespectfully?
- How do I handle the chores when differing visitation schedules mean we don't have the same children living in the house at any given time?
- How do I motivate a child who isn't expected to do anything at his other parent's house?
- As a single parent, how am I supposed to juggle everything: earn a living, go to school, get things done, and organize the children, too?
- How do I make sure I'm not expecting too much of the children?
- How do I deal with the pressure my ex puts on me to follow the same routines she does at her house so the children can experience consistency?
- What do I do if my child says she has to do all the work at her mother's house and doesn't think it's fair that she has to work at my house, too?
- What if my child is at her dad's house on the nights we choose our chores or create dinner menus and doesn't get a say?
- Is there a way to help my child remember what he needs to bring with him when he travels from home to home?

You may have already found ideas in *Chores without Wars* to help with these issues. In chapter 1, you learned about the importance of adjusting your attitude. That's especially helpful in a stepfamily situation. Realistic expectations make a huge difference between success and failure. The following thoughts are the most helpful: building a new team takes a lot of time and patience, the kids have a lot of adjustments to make, change is possible, and it would be foolish to take their behavior personally and turn normal reactions to change into power struggles.

In chapter 2, you learned about the six steps to winning family cooperation. They work extremely well in stepfamily and single-parent family situations, especially taking a step back and slowing down. The tricky part is clarifying who the coach is. A lot of popular wisdom says that the stepparent shouldn't be parenting someone else's children. When you use the ideas in this book, parenting is about creating teamwork in a respectful way. If that is what you are doing, you'll have few complaints from someone else's kids about what you are doing. You and your spouse can both participate in coaching your team.

Chapter 3 is one you could review over and over, because the more you are able to use good coaching strategies, the more you and your family members will succeed. If your family is experiencing difficulties in teamwork, you may not be valuing differences, inviting cooperation, using encouraging words, holding others accountable, or teaching skills. Time to go back to reviewing and practicing the basics.

Chapter 4 is all about helping family members make a transition. The suggestion is that you can allow a week for each change. With a stepfamily situation, you might need to modify that to a month, especially if the kids don't spend a lot of time at your place. It will be worth your efforts to change your expectations and slow down the process.

Chapter 5 is about routines, and routines will save you endless effort in a stepfamily situation. The children can learn that routines can vary from house to house, especially if you don't make comparisons or berate the other parent or insist on having the same routines at both homes. Children can adjust easily to different routines at different homes if you allow it and take time for training without being critical or judgmental.

In chapter 6, you learned how to make time in the kitchen enjoyable with your children. Spending time in the kitchen with stepchildren can build special relationships and be just as much fun. Letting your stepchildren cook a special meal or shop for foods they enjoy eating goes a long way to building team spirit.

Chapter 7, "The Art of Group Decision Making," is one of the best ways to coordinate and include stepchildren. That's why we spend a lot of time in this chapter showing you how well family meetings can work when the kids move back and forth.

What you learned about teens and money in chapters 8 and 9 applies to single-parent and stepparent situations with few differences. One of the worst things that you can do to your kids is put them in the middle when it comes to the money struggles you may be having with your ex. Those money issues shouldn't burden the children. They have enough to deal with without trying to run interference between you and your ex. Since the money issues seem to loom large in stepfamilies, we've added a special section in this chapter to help you deal with them.

In addition to what you can review in the previous chapters, we're offering further suggestions that specifically deal with changes that follow a divorce or other loss, like the death of a parent, or a parent leaving for any other reason. Even though these changes bring difficulties, the new family structure can also provide opportunities for creating new traditions and routines.

## COUNSELING IS SOMETIMES THE BEST SOLUTION FOR GETTING UNSTUCK

Due to the complexities of multiple relationships and increased stress from big changes, some families opt for outside help. There are programs in many communities to help stepfamilies and newly divorced parents, including parenting books that deal specifically with stepparent issues and parenting classes that raise awareness of what to do as a stepparent. Sometimes the best help can come from a family counselor who will teach your family skills for living and working together. That was the case for the Jordans. As you read their story, you can see why they needed nonjudgmental, outside help.

Gregory Jordan, a policeman and an avid athlete most of his life, was the king of locker room humor. On a family camping trip soon after he and his new wife, Lisa, were married, he played a prank on his twelve-year-old stepson Bernie. Bernie left his underwear on top of his sleeping bag in the tent. Gregory took a scoop of chili out of the cook pot, dumped it in the briefs, and left them in the middle of the campsite.

When Bernie saw his underwear, he ran from the campsite, humiliated. His mother ran after him while his fifteen-year-old step-sister, Dani, giggled in the background. When Lisa returned after talking to Bernie, she was furious. "Don't you ever treat my child like that again! I don't care how many times your teammates did that to you. My son doesn't think your pranks are funny, and neither do I. I don't think Bernie will ever recover."

Gregory was fuming. "Lisa, you're too soft. I think your son could be fun to be with, but you coddle him so much that he can't take a joke! And when I ask him to help out, he tells me I have no jurisdiction over him so he doesn't have to do what I say. I'm not willing to carry a help-less person. It's time Bernie shaped up and stopped being a baby."

"My son isn't a baby. Before we moved in with you, Bernie helped a lot. He was used to taking orders from me, but he doesn't want you telling him what to do. Now that you've humiliated him in public, I don't think he'll ever listen to you. I know Dani is used to your com-mands, but my son isn't going to do as you say."

"Lisa," Dani said, "I like the way my dad whipped me into shape. Before I moved in with him, I was lazy. He makes me do things, but I don't mind. Anyway, when you guys aren't around, Bernie does a lot of things to help out. I think he just doesn't want to help you, but when I ask him to do me a favor, he always says yes."

"I'm glad to hear that, Dani," Lisa replied, "but that doesn't change my feelings about your dad's relationship with Bernie. Gregory, if something needs to be done, I'll talk to Bernie. I want you to leave my son alone."

Gregory, Lisa, Dani, and Bernie were experiencing problems that often occur in blended families. Even though they share a home, they are tying themselves in knots and creating misunderstandings with rules about who can talk to whom and who is right or wrong.

After the camping trip, things went downhill for the Jordan family. Gregory was on Bernie all the time, despite Lisa's order that he leave her son alone. Lisa was so discouraged that she told Bernie to stop visiting until he agreed to help when Gregory asked. Bernie stopped coming to spend time with his mother and said he didn't care. Dani felt bad because she missed Bernie's visits. Because the Jordans felt stuck and didn't see a way out, they decided to seek counseling to get some help.

After they explained their situation to the counselor, she said, "I see this new family is bringing out issues for everyone. Since the two adults disagree on the way to parent, I suggest you try an entirely different method for making decisions in your new family, the family meeting."

At the suggestion of a family meeting, Gregory exclaimed, "I'd rather put an ice pick through my eye than attend a meeting."

"My, that's pretty extreme," replied the counselor, "but if you continue as you are now, I predict that Lisa, in her desperation to please you at the expense of her son, will become more resentful, Dani will turn into the family slave, Bernie will continue to get more angry and withdrawn, and you, Gregory, will become a tyrant. I don't think any of you wants that to happen."

"Of course we don't," said Lisa. "If Gregory and I learn something new together, I think it would work."

"Gregory," continued the counselor, "how would you feel about starting slowly to improve your relationship with Bernie? Perhaps you could ask if he would like to meet you at your club to shoot some baskets and work out? He might feel safer on neutral ground. Bernie's an athlete, and I bet you'd have a lot to show him. And Lisa, I think you need to let Gregory and Bernie know how painful this is for you. I bet you feel pulled in two different directions."

Lisa began to cry, and said, "These two guys are tearing me apart. I don't want to pick sides, but it feels like I'll lose my marriage if I allow Bernie to continue being so disrespectful to Gregory."

"Gregory and Lisa, if you would be willing to try my suggestions, I think we could include the children in our next session and learn how to hold family meetings. This is a time of adjustment for everyone. I realize you each did things differently before you got together, and that both of your methods worked. But now that you're all together, you'll need a plan you can agree on. If all of you would be willing to try some new things, the entire family would feel better." The Jordans agreed to try the counselor's suggestions before they did more damage to the relationships in the new family.

The Jordans aren't alone. Many families struggle with children who refuse to work or listen to a stepparent's requests simply because they don't want to be part of the new family. As the lack of cooperation increases, hurt feelings escalate. Instead of talking about their hurt feelings, stepparents often treat their stepchildren disrespectfully and further alienate each other. And some children feel taken advantage of because they are expected to do chores in two different households. Trying to work out the problems without the involvement of the children is extremely difficult. And trying to deal with such complex relationships without outside help can make solutions unattainable.

Not all situations are as extreme as the Jordans'. Many stepfamilies successfully institute family meetings or family talk times to figure out how to be a team.

## WORKING OUT STEPFAMILY CHORE PROBLEMS AT A FAMILY MEETING

Whatever happens in a family affects everyone in different ways. When Ben and Sarah joined their families in a second marriage, they never dreamed that they or the children would encounter so many issues about family jobs. Ben's children lived full time with Ben and Sarah. They were independent and involved with family chores. Eight-year-old Adam was used to helping without complaining.

Even two-year-old Francesca dressed herself and poured her own milk into her cereal from the miniature pitcher Ben provided for her.

Sarah's kids, fifteen-year-old Katie and ten-year-old Jonathan, lived with their father during the week and spent weekends with Ben and Sarah. When Sarah and her ex-husband Clint lived together, they had a maid and cleaning service. The children weren't expected to do any work at all. After the divorce, Clint quit his job to start a new business, which meant a big decrease in income. Clint expected his children to take care of the household chores while he developed his new business. After many difficulties during the five years following the divorce, the children took on more and more work around his house.

One weekend when Katie and Jonathan were at Ben and Sarah's place, Ben insisted they help with the yard work. He was tired of watching them relax while his children worked. Both Katie and Jonathan ignored Ben. Katie ran to her mother and said, "Ben just told us we have to help with the yard work. This isn't even our house. Just because you decided to marry Ben doesn't mean we're going to do what he says. He's not our father."

Sarah told her children, "I know Ben isn't your father, but he is a person who lives in this house and has rights just like the rest of us. I think of this house as belonging to everyone, even if you don't see it that way. I'm sorry you're so angry. I can't make you help, but I'd feel a lot better if you could contribute when you're here." Katie stopped complaining, but she and Jonathan refused to help with the yard work and went inside to watch a video.

Ben continued to feel resentful. He didn't ask the children to help any more that day, but he complained vehemently to Sarah about how "spoiled" and "irresponsible" her children were. It hurt Sarah to hear Ben talk that way. She felt upset because she didn't think her children were spoiled or irresponsible and she wanted Ben to be happy.

After Sarah's children returned to their father's, Adam asked his father, "How come Sarah's kids never have to do chores when they stay with us? It's not fair that we have to do all the work around here." Ben agreed it wasn't fair, but said that Sarah's kids refused to listen to him and Sarah wasn't going to do anything about it.

Sarah overheard the conversation. "Adam," she said, "you sound pretty angry about this."

"I sure am," he said. "Why don't you make your kids help out?"

Sarah thought for a moment and said, "I don't want to insist they work if they don't want to. I know they do a lot all week at their dad's house, and I think they need a break on weekends."

"I think you're just afraid they'll stop coming over if you ask them to help," argued Ben. "Maybe I should go on strike and refuse to do anything for your kids until they pitch in around here."

Adam liked that idea, but Sarah said, "I know you're angry and I'm upset that my kids are being disrespectful, too, but that's too extreme! Ben, you may be right that I'm afraid the kids will stop coming over if I push more work on them, and you do have the right to expect cooperation. Instead of a strike, how about if we sit down as a family the next time they come and talk about what is happening?"

The next time Sarah's children were at the house, everyone sat down to discuss the chore problem. Sarah started the meeting by telling her children that Ben was so upset with their behavior that he was considering going on strike and refusing to help them until they decided to help the family. "I'm not in favor of a strike, but I also don't think it's right for us to do all the work. I would like to understand why you don't help when you're here. In fact, I think everyone in the family should have a chance to say what they think about this problem."

Adam spoke first. "I'm glad we're having a meeting. I'm really mad that I have to do so much work around here. Francesca is only two and can't do very many things yet, so I get stuck with everything. I don't think it's fair that you guys don't help when you're here. Sometimes when you leave, Sarah expects me to clean up your messes and that's not right. And I don't like sharing my bedroom with you, Jonathan, because you leave your stuff everywhere when you go back to your dad's."

Katie said, "I don't think it's fair that you have to clean up after us, Adam. I'll make sure I pick up my things before I leave. But Ben, we have to work all week at Dad's house. We never get a break. Then when we come here and it's our weekend, you have a million things for us to do. We don't want to work all the time just because you do!"

"Yeah," said Jonathan, "but Adam, I'm sorry about leaving your room all messy. I wouldn't like someone doing that to my room."

Ben spoke up, "I have an idea. Are we ready for a solution?" Everyone nodded in agreement. "I do like to get a lot done on weekends, but I don't expect you to work the whole time you're here. How about each of you giving me an hour a day? I promise not to bug you the rest of the weekend." Sarah let out a sigh of relief. This was the first time she heard Ben be reasonable. She was so worried that her children wouldn't want to come for weekends if they couldn't resolve this issue. She wanted to support Ben, but she thought he was expecting too much of the children.

Katie said an hour a day would be fine as long as she and Ben planned the time together so it didn't interfere with her part-time job, her boyfriend, or her homework. Jonathan thought an hour a day would be fun if he and Adam could work together. Ben assured the children he could schedule the work to meet their needs.

Two-year-old Francesca, who had been sitting quietly during the discussion, asked, "More ice cream?" Sarah and Ben exchanged smiles of relief, knowing their combined family had taken a first step toward more harmonious living.

## COORDINATING SCHEDULES: A CHALLENGE FOR STEPFAMILIES

Sometimes the problem isn't whether family members are willing to help, but rather whether they are available to help. In some families, members are rarely in the same place at the same time because of varying visitation schedules and active lifestyles. Sometimes finding ways to share the workload and create times everyone can work together just isn't possible.

If you are having a problem with schedules, try these tips:

1.  *Use signs, notes, and other nonverbal ways to make requests.* A creative mother made a special envelope for each child with his or her name and photo on it. When the child was at the house, he or she found chore assignments inside the envelope. A family that used a large erasable board to notify family members of work assignments told the following story: "When we painted the inside of the house, all our routines fell apart for days. We thought it was because of the painting until our eight-year-old stepdaughter arrived for the weekend. She asked, 'Where's our erase board? I can't remember if I'm supposed to cook tonight or tomorrow.' We hadn't realized how much we depended on looking at the board to remind us of chores and routines. We put everything on that board—doctor's appointments, shopping lists, menu choices, car pool days, music lessons, sports events, the works. We put the board back up before we hung our pictures so we could get back to normal."

2.  *Create family work days once a month.* You can usually find one day a month when everyone can get together. Make sure you have fun, too. Play lively music and plan a pizza party or ice cream sundae treat at the end of the day.

3.  *Agree on the amount of time each family member will work during the week and let each person work at his or her convenience.* This works best if you keep a chart of the job, who is going to do it, when they plan to do it, and when it will be completed. It also helps to get pre-agreement about ways you can give nonverbal reminders if the job falls through the cracks. The easiest almost nonverbal reminder is to ask the person assigned to the job, "Could you check our chart and see who

agreed to vacuum the family room?" That almost always gets the job done.

4. *Assign work by the percentage of time spent in the family.* For example, if a stepchild stays at the house 10 percent of the time, he or she would be expected to contribute 10 percent of a full-time work share.

5. *Consider whether or not the job can wait until the person returns.* If the job can't wait, the person whose job it is can arrange in advance to have another family member fill in. Someone can offer to do the job for the absent family member if that person is willing to make a trade or do something extra when he or she returns to the house. Sometimes family members are willing to do extra jobs for pay when negotiated in advance.

6. *Consider including the position of "alternate" in job planning.* The alternate fills in and does the jobs for absent family members for an agreed period of time. Set this up during the regular job-planning process.

7. *Try a check system.* One family decided together that if a person forgot a chore before leaving for the other parent's home, he or she would get a check. After accumulating three checks, the person would do extra dishes for everyone the next time he or she was at the house.

8. *Set up a "switch" basket.* Give each child who moves from home to home a special basket where they can put items or clothing that they need to take with them when they leave. Before they make the switch, remind them to check their switch basket. It's a lot easier than having to hunt down items throughout the house or make endless trips to pick up or deliver forgotten items.

As long as everyone agrees in advance, a system will usually work. If there are problems, put them on the agenda for the next family meeting.

Three other reasons often make inviting cooperation difficult. Perhaps one family member (or more) refuses to help at all because work isn't expected at his or her other home. Still others simply don't know how to do a job and are embarrassed to admit it. In other cases, children may feel competitive and refuse to do anything another family member can do better.

## MOTIVATING A CHILD WHO IS NOT USED TO HELPING OUT

Making work a game can motivate an untrained, unskilled worker to get involved and make a contribution. Remember the story in chapter 3 where Beck's thirteen-year-old stepson Keith was a frequent dinner guest at the house, but consistently disappeared when it was time to help? Keith was too embarrassed to admit he didn't know how to do much around the house. Rather than humiliate him further, Beck used humor to invite participation, and it worked well.

There are other reasons someone won't help out. Sometimes it's a simple case of sibling rivalry, even though the siblings can be from different parents. That's what happened in another stepfamily situation where Louise refused to cook when at her father's house because her stepsister Susan made fun of her and criticized her efforts. Susan was an excellent cook who got compliments on everything she made, but felt threatened by competition. Louise, figuring she couldn't compete, said she hated cooking and refused to help with that chore. At her mother's house, however, Louise cooked almost every day to avoid her mother's specialties: fried foods, gravies, grade "D" meats—anything high in fat. Louise was taking a nutrition class at her high school and didn't want to eat foods her teacher said were unhealthy.

One weekend the two girls decided to stay home together while their parents attended an out of town conference. While Susan slept in on Saturday, Louise cooked her favorite spinach, bacon, and mushroom omelet for breakfast. As the cooking smells wafted up the stairs,

Susan couldn't stop herself from coming down to check out what was for breakfast. When she saw and smelled the puffy omelet, she said, "Busted! I thought you said you couldn't cook? I'll keep my mouth shut for half of that omelet."

"I'll give you half of this omelet if you stop acting like you're the only person in the world who can cook." Susan thought for a minute and then said, "You're on. Sorry!"

Stepfamilies aren't the only ones with problems to solve. Single parents tell us they are overwhelmed and exhausted trying to juggle everything. Even if it was only an illusion, they thought they had someone to turn to for help before their divorce or death of a spouse. Now they find living alone with the children isolating and difficult.

## OTHER ISSUES SINGLE PARENTS STRUGGLE WITH

If you are a single parent, do you worry that your children have to grow up too fast because of the extra responsibilities you give them to help make the family work? Do you sometimes find it easier to do everything yourself because teaching the children a new routine takes too long? Do you feel overwhelmed most of the time because there's just too much for one person to do? Do you occasionally take this out on your children?

Jim, a single father of two, sixteen-year-old Sammy, and fourteen-year-old Jane, struggled with these issues. Jim's two teens lived with him except for occasional visits with their mother, who took them on trips to fabulous resorts or on special fun outings such as sporting events and concerts. In an effort to make sure his children learned to be responsible, Jim created a routine that worked smoothly, except for minor irritations when one child felt the work was divided unevenly. Usually problems were discussed at family meetings, and everyone helped solve them.

Jim's routine changed when his company sent him back to school to retrain for a new program. After working all day, attending classes in the evenings, and trying to keep up with his homework, he had no patience for problem solving or family meetings. He snapped at his children and insisted they take on extra work because he was too busy. He resented the time his children spent with their mother, because they were off having fun while he was home slaving away.

Jane and Sammy were responsible and did their best to help out, but Jim's expectations were impossible. The teens, tired of trying to pick up the slack, decided to write a letter to their dad, when they couldn't pin him down for family meeting.

After debating what to write, Jane and Sammy composed the following letter and gave it to their father.

*Dear Dad,*

*We want to help you out, but you are taking advantage of us. We wish you had a wife to help you with the extra work. We think you are dumping everything on us because we are the only ones here. You are putting too much on us. When you ask us to do your jobs, we get frustrated because we can't say no and argue with you. Then we all get in some kind of fight about something little or just don't talk for about two or three hours. It happens practically every day, and although we try to be nice, we can't be because you treat us like slaves.*

*We could work this problem out together if we had a family meeting, but since you are too busy to meet with us, we have three ideas. They are better than nothing at all or us being mad at each other all the time.*

*Our first suggestion is that when you come in the house, you should say "hi" before you start giving us a list of things to do. Our second suggestion is that we could have a counseling session to figure out a way for us to stop getting on each other's nerves. Our third suggestion is that maybe we could set a work time on the weekend when we could help each other with the extra jobs.*

*All of these solutions can work very well, but we all need to agree on what we will do, because your tone of voice and timing just isn't going to*

*work. We definitely can't keep going on like we are now, always coming home annoying each other all the time. It just doesn't work. We hope you can agree with one of these choices. Maybe we can talk about this soon.*
*Love always,*
*Jane and Sammy*

When Jim read the letter, he realized he had lost sight of what a parent's role is and what a child's is. He knew he had been ordering his teens around because he was so stressed. He didn't think what he was doing was fair, but he was desperate because he couldn't think of anyone else to ask for help. Jim realized that he had been thinking only of himself. He decided to take a break from his homework and talk with his children.

After apologizing for his behavior, Jim asked if he could add some suggestions to the list the children had started.

"Great, Dad. All we want to do is solve the problem. What are your ideas?"

Jim said, "We could agree on an amount of time each person would work during the week, do what we can, and let the rest go. Or maybe we could hire someone to do my chores."

"Dad, you know you can't afford to hire someone. How about we each put in an hour a week whenever we have time, and then we could work together for an hour on the weekend to finish what is left," suggested Sammy.

"Great idea. Let's do it. And thanks for writing me such a great letter. Your old dad seems to have gone temporarily insane, but I'll get better with your help." Everyone laughed.

Then Sammy said, "Dad, we know how busy you are, but we miss having fun with you like we used to. Remember when we played 'Make-Me-Laugh' at the dinner table? That didn't take much time, but it was fun trying to get everybody to laugh. Remember the time Jane and I wouldn't laugh until you poured syrup over your head? We didn't stop laughing for a week. Could we play that again soon?"

"How about right now?" Jim started making faces.

"Come on, Dad," said Jane, "you can do better than that!"

It's easy to take advantage of capable children when you are a single parent. Even if you don't want your children to assume all the work, it's tempting to allow it when you are at work or involved in activities away from home. Your children may even be more skilled at doing housework than you are, because they were more involved before the divorce or death. Remember that they are just kids and it's not their job to pick up your slack.

Another difficulty for single parents is working things out with their ex-partner. Sometimes two people who were married can be friends who cooperate in the interest of the children. Other times there is no communication at all. And in most cases, there are difficulties and disagreements to work out.

## WORKING OUT ISSUES WITH EX-PARTNERS

Brad's ex-wife Wendy ran her home like an army barracks. When the children stayed with their father, Wendy called regularly to insist that Brad follow the routines she did. She pushed all his guilt buttons when she said the children were confused by the inconsistencies.

Brad didn't want to make it hard for his children, so he tried to do things the way Wendy did. Wendy wanted Brad to give the children allowance only if they did all their work. Brad didn't think it was a good idea to connect chores with money. He thought it was a better idea to pay the children for extra jobs he would hire someone to do and give them their allowance so they could learn to deal with money. But Wendy insisted that, even though they were divorced, his job as a father was to help her parent the children consistently so they didn't get confused.

One morning Brad's daughter refused to clear the table. Although she was running late, she didn't like the outfit she picked and wanted to change before the school bus came. "You look just fine the way you are," said Brad. "If you don't clear the table, I'm deducting money from your allowance."

"That's not fair. You said we could have an allowance to buy things we need. Besides, taking it away is punishment, and you said you don't believe in punishment."

"I don't care what I said, just clear that table and stop arguing."

"No, I won't. I don't care if you give me an allowance or not. I'm going to change my clothes and catch the bus."

Brad felt miserable all day because of the fight with his daughter. He couldn't concentrate on a thing at work. During a coffee break, Brad told a coworker about Wendy's demands and his fight with their daughter.

"Brad," she asked, "do you think our competitors do everything exactly the way we do in our company?"

"Of course not. We all have different ways of operating." Brad paused then added, "Oh, I get it. Are you saying it's okay if Wendy does things her way and I do things my way?"

"Of course it is," said his friend. "Your differences were probably one of the reasons you and Wendy didn't stay together. Now you have your own place and you need to find out what works for you."

Brad heaved a sigh of relief. He couldn't believe he had lost sight of such a simple truth. He called his ex-wife. "Wendy, I've been thinking about something. Every family has different rules and different ways of doing things. At your house you do things your way, and that's your business. But at my house, I've been trying to do things your way, too, and it isn't working for me. From now on, I'm going to do things my way at my house. The kids will figure out that there are different ways to do things and won't be confused if you and I don't criticize each other."

"Brad, parents must present a united front or their children will be permanently damaged," argued Wendy.

"I know you have the best interests of the children in mind, but I don't agree with what you are saying. It would be better for all of us if you would stop pressuring me to do things your way. That's not a good message for the children. We have two different houses now and two different families and two different ways of doing things. I know it may take a little time to make the transition, but our children are very capable, and they'll work it out." Brad wasn't sure if Wendy liked his suggestion, but he was certain that it was all right to be himself with his children.

When his daughter came home later that day, he asked, "When did you start feeling better after our fight this morning? I've been miserable all day."

She smiled and said, "I stopped being mad as soon as I got on the bus with my friends, but I still don't think it's right for you to punish me by taking away my allowance."

"I agree with you. I was under a lot of pressure this morning, and I made a mistake threatening you like that. I'm not going to take away your allowance."

Brad's daughter gave him a big hug and said, "Did you clear the table for me this morning? Maybe I could do your job tonight."

"That would be really nice," said Brad.

Even with pressure from Wendy, Brad decided to focus on what worked for him. Change is a slow process, and Brad made mistakes along the way, but he was capable of learning from his errors when no one was standing on the sidelines judging him.

## PUTTING KIDS IN THE MIDDLE OF THE MONEY MUDDLE

Kids don't belong in the middle of your divorce. Every time you criticize one of their parents, you're pulling off a scab on a painful event that rarely heals if the kids are supposed to pick a side. Nothing prevents healing like using the kids as a pawn regarding money.

Tracy never knew where she stood when her parents argued about money. She loved both of her parents, but she didn't agree with how they dealt with each other. She thought her mother was childlike about money, so when she was at her mom's house, she tried not to ask for anything or need anything that cost money. She was afraid if she did, her mom might not be able to pay her rent. When she was with her dad, she tried not to need anything because her dad constantly complained that he had to pay for everything because her mother was such an irresponsible spendthrift.

Neither parent gave Tracy an allowance. Her mother expected her to do a lot of work around the house because, as she said, "I have to do everything by myself, unlike your father who has a wife to take care of him. You have to help me, because you're the only person I can count on." Her father gave Tracy money whenever she asked for it, but always accompanied it with, "It's too bad your mother can't take any responsibility to pay for your needs."

Being on the outside, you can see how the parents were pulling Tracy apart. Her father's friend Milt saw what was going on and told Tracy's dad, Ed, he wanted to talk to him about Tracy. Ed agreed to meet him for coffee.

"Ed," Milt said, "I know you love Tracy and you've taken care of her financially since she was a baby. But you are killing that kid by putting her mother down."

"Milt, you know Sue. She's totally irresponsible. We're stretched to the limit with Tracy's needs and all Sue can ever think of is how to get more child support out of me. I can't understand what I ever saw in her. The best thing we ever did was have Tracy."

"Ed, you're right about Tracy. Do yourself a favor and stop tormenting the girl. Sit down with her and find out what her expenses are and give her an allowance. Stop giving her money with so many strings attached. And get the girl helping around the house. She's becoming a martyr, like her mother. She needs to have some chores and some responsibility," Milt said.

Although Ed felt that Tracy already had too much responsibility at her mom's house, he agreed with Milt's points. He started giving Tracy an allowance, stopped putting her mom down, and gave her a list of three chores he expected her to do each day. Although she grumbled about not having enough time, he realized that she had plenty of time. In fact, she stopped wasting a lot of time, because now she had some real responsibility. When Tracy came to him and said she needed a new pair of jeans, he suggested she save from her allowance. When she came home and told him her mom bought her a pair of designer jeans and now couldn't afford the rent, he said, "Tracy, that's between you and your mom. I'm sure she'll figure it out." Tracy was shocked that he didn't use that as an opportunity to complain about how irresponsible her mom was. She loved her jeans and she didn't want to worry about whether her mom could afford them or not. For the first time in years, Tracy didn't think she had to act the part of the parent with her mom, which was a huge relief.

## MISTAKES: WONDERFUL OPPORTUNITIES TO LEARN AND GROW

Ed, and many parents who've been divorced, make a lot of mistakes. That is what they are—mistakes. If they knew another way to handle situations or were aware of what they were doing, they might do things differently. Anyone can make a mistake, but it takes courage and conviction to learn from them. When you or your children meet the challenges of divorce or death, you can learn to handle whatever life presents with courage and optimism. If you remember to focus on progress instead of perfection, you will be amazed at how well your family can handle the aftereffects of divorce or death. There's no rush. Just let the process unfold and use the suggestions in this chapter (and the rest of the book) to help you through the rough spots.

# 11

# DEALING WITH ADULT
# LIVING SITUATIONS
# YOU NEVER IMAGINED

When you think about chores, you're probably thinking about families with school-age children. This chapter offers help to those of you who are adjusting to living with an empty nest, who live with kids moving in and out of the house, or with children who don't want to leave home. We also offer ideas for those families who find themselves faced with the responsibility of caring for an elderly parent in their home, or for those who live in a roommate situation. We explore how to deal with an abusive situation in your own home, although we hope that you will never have the need to use this information.

Creating teamwork and solving problems will be easier if you are fortunate enough to live with people who are motivated to cooperate. If you are the only person who wants improvement, your work will be more difficult, but you can use the ideas in the early chapters of this book to learn to invite others to cooperate. Because we believe that a home should be safe and comfortable for all family members, we offer alternatives to putting up with uncomfortable or disrespectful situations.

## WHAT TO DO WHEN THE KIDS MOVE OUT

Trudy started attending parenting classes when Ali was three and Mary was five. She and her husband, Chuck, often attended classes together and worked hard to teach the girls new skills. Over the years each used the five coaching strategies recommended in chapter 3 and the family established a cooperative way of handling the household work. They really were a team, even through their children's adolescence.

When Mary left for college, the family had to reevaluate their situation and make adjustments. The household tasks that Mary handled had to be reassigned. Chuck, Trudy, and Ali realized that with their team shrinking, they would each have to take on more. Chuck volunteered to get take-out food on Tuesdays, the night Mary had made dinner. Ali said she'd be willing to clean the upstairs bathroom on cleaning day and set the table on the nights she was home.

Trudy told them she appreciated their team spirit. She offered to feed their dog Squirt and handle the trips to the vet. They all realized how much each family member was contributing to make their household run smoothly.

When Ali moved into an apartment two years later, Trudy and Chuck found themselves having to adjust once again. They decided how they could divide things up so neither was overburdened. Chuck took on another night to cook dinner and they decided to go out once a week. Trudy said she'd set the table. Since both Trudy and Chuck worked full time, they decided to hire someone to clean the house. Trudy jokingly remarked that having the girls leave was hard since she and Chuck had come to rely on their help to keep the family running. With experienced team players like their daughters, things seemed to happen automatically.

When Mary and Ali came home for visits, Trudy and Chuck noticed that everyone naturally fell into the family routines set up a long time before. Mary set the table before dinner; after the meal, Ali cleared the table just like when she had lived at home. Trudy beamed, realizing that the years of training and working together really had paid off.

One night Trudy and Chuck rushed out to an early movie, leaving the kitchen a mess. They returned to find their daughters, who had come for a visit, chattering away about their work and friends as they stood at the kitchen sink washing their parents' dinner dishes. Chuck asked, "What's going on?" Ali replied, "The dishes were piled up and we knew you'd be back late, so Mary and I thought we'd do them for you." Chuck gave his girls a big hug and thanked them profusely.

Mary and Ali moved into their own places after leaving home and didn't come back to live in the household. Some children who leave home do return after a while. In fact, one family had grown children coming and going so often that they joked about installing a revolving door. Many children spend summers or vacations living with their family, between college semesters or seasonal jobs. Some children return home to save money for an adventure or a place of their own.

## THE REVOLVING DOOR: WHEN CHILDREN COME AND GO

After a year of sharing an apartment with his friend, Clark decided to move back home with his parents for a few months to catch up on his bills. Clark moved back into his old room and into old habits. He "borrowed" things from his dad, like clothes or tools, and didn't return them. He made a lot of promises to pitch in and help, but he didn't follow through on what he said he'd do. He acted more like a guest than a participating family member.

Clark asked to borrow his dad's car one Friday night. As his father debated whether to let Clark use his car, Clark said, "I'll wash it this weekend. Looks like it could use it." Miles decided to let him use the car, but on Monday morning when he left for work, he noticed it was still dirty.

The next day as Miles was getting ready for work, he said to his wife, "I can't find my brown belt. Do you know where it is?"

"No, but I saw your son wearing it yesterday."

Her husband said, "I can't believe he took my belt. Why does he borrow my things? He never washed the car like he said he would either. I can't trust him, and I'm sick of this. I'm going to have to talk to that boy."

Like Miles, "I trusted you!" is what people say who feel their trust has been betrayed. We suggest you trust people to be who they are instead of living in hope that the person will be someone else. Miles was disappointed and hoped his son would behave differently. His wife offered to call her cousin Bernice to see how she handled a similar problem with her son a few years back.

Bernice was glad to share her solution. Whenever her son borrowed something, she asked for collateral, that is, something he needed or something that was important to him. She kept it until the borrowed item was returned, which she said was usually when promised. Miles decided to try her idea out with his son.

The following day Clark asked to borrow his dad's brown sweater, promising to return it the next morning. Miles said, "I want some collateral first."

Clark asked, "What do you mean?"

"Give me your favorite CD. I'll keep it until I get my sweater back," his father replied.

The next day Clark asked his dad for his CD and handed him his brown sweater, along with the belt he had borrowed earlier that week.

By asking for collateral, Miles trusted Clark to be who he was and developed a plan to take care of himself. He continued to use collateral whenever Clark borrowed something from him. On one occasion he had collected his son's left dress shoe, car keys, and address book.

Even though Miles was working out some improvements with his son, he was not happy with how comfortable Clark had become living back at home. He knew that Clark wasn't planning to be part of the family team. He still left his dirty dishes and wrappers on the living room table. He wasn't paying his bills or saving money.

Miles and Louise realized that it was time to set limits on how long Clark could stay and decided to sit down to talk with him and express their concern.

"Clark," his father began, "your mother and I love you enough to set a limit on how long you can stay here. We don't think we're helping you be responsible by providing free maid service and room and board, so we'd like you to find another place by the end of the month. If you need our help, we'll be glad to go looking for places with you."

Clark responded by saying he was planning a move soon anyway, and it was okay. They asked Clark if he would like his old furniture, either to use or to sell so he could buy something for his new place.

When Clark got settled in his new place, his folks redecorated his old room as a combination guest room (kids could visit for a maximum of three days) and study. Louise moved her computer in and Miles set up his aquarium. Clark was shocked to see his room dismantled, but he knew his parents were right to do it.

## WHEN ADULT CHILDREN REFUSE TO LEAVE HOME

Clark was willing to move but sometimes that isn't the case, especially when your child is comfortable at home or doesn't have a job and doesn't want to move out. Jeanine was a single mom. Her son, Boyd, was twenty-four and her daughter, Sally, was nineteen. Boyd was away at graduate school and Sally was living at home after a semester at the junior college. She was tired of going to school and said that she needed a break. She told Jeanine she'd get a job and work for a while.

Although Sally told her mom that she was going to get a job, she went out with friends at night and she spent her days getting up late and lying on the couch watching TV. Although she used to participate in the family work, now she left food out in the kitchen, crumbs on the counters, and dirty dishes on the coffee table. Jeanine would come home from work and say, "What did you do all day? This place is a mess. You never used to be like this. All you do is watch TV. What's wrong?"

This time, Sally got off the couch and yelled, "You're always on my case. It's no big deal." She gathered up the dishes and did a half-hearted cleanup.

Jeanine said, "We have to talk. You can't live your life this way. Either get a job or go to school."

Sally went into her room and left a few minutes later.

Jeanine felt like she was getting to the end of her rope. She loved Sally but was starting not to like her. Sally was turning twenty in a month and Jeanine didn't want to live this way any longer. Jeanine talked to Sally the following day and although Sally said she would look for work, her behavior didn't change. Jeanine finally told her daughter she'd have to move out. Sally thought she could share a place with a friend but when that fell through, Sally simply told her mother, "I have nowhere to go. I have to stay here."

Jeanine realized that she couldn't make Sally do anything. She'd have to decide what she'd do since her daughter was refusing to move out. Sally's refusal to take on the responsibility of managing her own life put her mom in the position of having to make a difficult decision. Jeanine talked with her friend Madeline to get some objective perspective.

Madeline agreed that Jeanine would have to focus on what she would do. She shared that she had charged her own son rent (lower than market rate) and that had motivated him to get his own place.

Since Sally didn't have a job, they realized that probably wouldn't improve things. One of Madeline's friends had, after setting a deadline to be out, actually packed up his son's things, put them out on the porch, and changed the locks. That got his son out, but that felt too drastic to Jeanine. She realized she'd have to come up with something she could follow through on.

She finally decided that her lease was up in two months and she told Sally that she was moving out and finding a smaller place. Sally was not invited to join her. At first Sally was shocked and was sure her Mom would let her move with her. But as she watched her Mom lease a small one-bedroom apartment and start the packing process, Sally believed that Jeanine was serious. As moving day approached, Sally told her mother she'd be staying with a friend for a few weeks and was actively filling out job applications.

Jeanine said, "Sally, I have faith in you to work things out. If and when you decide to go back to school, I'd like to pay for your tuition and books. In the meantime, stop by for dinner any Sunday you like."

It was difficult for Miles and Louise to ask Clark to leave and for Jeanine to have Sally move out. Parents have a right to live without children and should not feel obligated to continue providing for them when they become adults. If you want to help your adult children for a short time but do not want them to become permanent household residents and dependent on you, let them know your limitations before they move in. If you enjoy having your adult children live with you, make sure you establish a way to work out difficulties together and to clarify agreements instead of operating by assumptions and innuendo.

## THE CHALLENGE OF ADDING YOUR AGING PARENTS TO YOUR HOME

Adult children aren't the only ones who are moving back home these days. People live longer today than ever before, and the average life expectancy continues to increase. That leaves many middle-aged children asking the question "What will happen to my parents? Will I ever have one or both of them living with me?" In the coming years, many of you will answer yes.

Whether you find yourself living under the same roof with an elderly parent because of financial circumstances, health reasons, or because you want to, many issues are bound to come up. How you handle these situations is critical to the relationship you'll have with your parent. Living with an aging parent can be either a difficult and frustrating experience or a rich and rewarding one.

Carl Kassel had three sons and a daughter, Ethel. Carl and his sons lived in Wisconsin, and Ethel lived in California. Ethel got calls from her brothers periodically saying their dad was having increasing difficulty living alone. Finally her oldest brother called to say he and the other brothers had decided it would be best for Carl to move to California and live with Ethel. "After all," he said, "you are his daughter and we've looked after him all these years."

Ethel told her husband, Harley, what her brother had said. She was feeling guilty about being so far away from her father all these years and wanted him to come to live with them. Although he had his reservations because Carl was not an easy man, Harley agreed.

Carl and his black lab, Bounder, moved in with Ethel and Harley and proceeded to make themselves at home. Carl sat in front of the TV most of the time and expected Ethel to wait on him. Bounder whined at the door for hours, but Carl just yelled at him to shut up instead of walking him. Since the Hopkinses' yard wasn't fenced in, Bounder had nowhere to run without supervision. Harley felt so sorry for the dog that he started taking him on daily walks. Ethel worked full time and did most of the cooking, cleaning, and shopping. Harley would help out when asked. Carl expressed no interest in helping around the house and treated Ethel like she was the maid. He was extremely critical to boot.

A few months after he arrived, Carl was exceptionally vocal at dinner one night. "Ethel, what did you do to this meat? I can't chew it. You know I hate broccoli, and these potatoes are runny. I can't eat this stuff." Ethel burst into tears.

"Now what are you crying about?" Carl continued, "You're just like your mother. You cry at the drop of a hat." He got up and left the table.

Harley tried to comfort his wife and said, "You don't deserve to be treated this way."

Ethel said, "I can't take this anymore. I do his laundry, cook, and clean. All he does is complain and criticize. Yesterday I asked if he could at least wash out his coffee cup. By the look he gave me, you'd think I committed a crime. He doesn't do anything to help out, even when I ask him to."

Ethel called her older brother and told him things weren't working out.

"I was afraid this might happen. I'll call the other brothers and get back to you," he said. They all agreed to chip in to cover the cost of an apartment in a retirement community where Carl could be provided with the services he required.

Perhaps even under the best of circumstances, Ethel and Harley would have been unable or unwilling to deal with Carl. Had they considered the tips on the following list, though, they may have been able to create a more workable situation with Carl. We recommend that you consider the following five strategies before adding an elderly parent to your home.

1. Be clear about your boundaries. What jobs are you willing and able to do, what jobs need to be hired out (including nursing care), and what do you expect your parent to do? What are your guidelines for pets, smoking, drinking, and visitors? How much room is there for negotiation about these requirements?
2. Be clear about defining space. What rooms are available to your parent? Where and when will family members watch TV? What routines does the family have that won't be changing (such as overnights with friends, birthday parties, trips away from home)?

3. Set up a forum, such as a weekly family meeting, for sharing and working out problems and handling complaints and criticism. Make sure your parent knows he or she will be invited to be part of family decision making and that his or her input is important.

4. Find out your parent's special skills and focus on positive ways for him or her to be involved and significant in the family. Let your parent know where he or she can help pick up the slack or trade services. Be clear with your parent that he or she will be a valued team member, not a guest, in your household.

5. Create activities the family can do together for fun and closeness. Include new rituals and routines like a special dinner once a week or an outing on weekends or a day to look through picture albums together. Get input from your parent about activities he or she enjoys that the family could join.

The Harris family was able to use many of the tips on the list, thus creating ways for Clare's mother-in-law to fit in and become part of the team and not a disruption to the entire family. Clare and Walter Harris had two children—Martin, nineteen, and Helen, seventeen. Martin was away at college and Helen was starting her senior year. Clare and Walter had talked about moving to a smaller house after Helen graduated from high school. They wondered why they should keep a large house just for two of them.

Irene, Walter's seventy-eight-year-old mother, had lived alone for the past seven years after her husband died. She was independent and kept herself busy with her interests and activities. While visiting Irene, Clare noticed some alarming changes in her mother-in-law. Once an excellent housekeeper, Irene seemed to be slowing down. Clare noticed a grime buildup in the bathroom, the kitchen garbage filled to overflowing, and dirty dishes stacked at the sink. Some of the "clean" dishes in the cupboard looked as if they could use a going over. Clare washed the dishes and took the garbage to the Dumpster on her way to the car. She decided to talk with her husband that evening and share her concerns.

"Honey," Clare began, "I'm very concerned about your mother."

"What do you mean?" Walter asked.

"I stopped by to see her and noticed her house isn't the way she used to keep it. The tub was grimy, the garbage was overflowing, and the dishes were dirty. That's just not like her. I don't think she can really take care of herself anymore."

Helen overheard their conversation and added, "I stopped by Gram's last week and she told me the same story three times. At first I thought she was fooling around, but she really didn't know she was repeating herself."

Walter thought for a little while then sighed. "So what are you saying?"

Clare said, "It's becoming harder for your mother to live alone. Let's be realistic and face facts, and think about what we can do."

"She'll never go into one of those homes for old people. She said she'd die first."

Clare responded, "I'm not talking about a nursing home, but we have to deal with this and consider our options."

A few weeks later when Irene was visiting with the Harrises she asked, "What are you going to do when Helen leaves for school? This is such a big house for just the two of you."

Clare replied, "Oh, I don't know. We were talking about moving into something smaller."

"Oh." Irene sighed and then got quiet. Later that night Walter remarked, "I wonder what my mother meant by that comment about our house."

"Do you think she was hinting that she'd like to live here? You know how hard it is for your mother to be direct."

"How do you feel about my mother moving in? Is it even a possibility?"

"I suppose so. The house is large and we could fix up the downstairs room for your mom." After more discussion they got input from the kids and were ready to talk to Irene.

Initially she was reluctant, but she decided to make the move after she found out her good friend was being placed in a nursing home. They talked together about what Irene should bring, where they could put her things, and what items could be sold at a garage sale. Irene moved into a comfortable room and had many familiar items around to help her feel more at home. The Harrises involved her in their regularly scheduled family meetings and encouraged her to put items on the agenda. They decided to have a cleaning day on Saturdays. Helen liked to sleep in, so they set the work time from 10:00 a.m. to 2:00 p.m.

As the family was doing the Saturday cleaning, Clare noticed her mother-in-law was looking tired as she pushed the vacuum. "Mom, why don't you switch with me and sit and fold the towels. I could use a break." Irene sat down and folded for fifteen minutes, which allowed her to catch her breath. She got up and began dusting, swaying to the beat of Helen's new CD.

Walter did the family's grocery shopping on Mondays. He asked his mother to help him with it because she always picked out such wonderful produce. While they were out, he noticed Irene was looking tired. Walter suggested they take a break and get some frozen yogurt. After the break, Irene was able to continue shopping. Irene didn't have the stamina and energy she once did, but she wouldn't speak up for fear of inconveniencing her family. Walter and Clare were sensitive to this and planned accordingly.

Helen was scheduled to cook one evening when she noticed her grandmother sitting in her room. "Gram, would you tell me how to cook those wonderful mashed potatoes you used to make?"

Irene went into the kitchen with Helen and started rattling off the ingredients and explained how to prepare the potatoes.

Helen was excited. "Would you be willing to work with me on my night to cook and teach me how to make all the things I loved to eat at your house?"

Irene beamed and said, "Of course. I'll get the ingredients when I go shopping with your dad."

"Great! Can we make that great manicotti I loved? We could surprise Mom and Dad with it for dinner."

The Harrises found many opportunities to help Irene feel like a member of the team, important, useful, and appreciated. They looked for ways to involve her in the household work so she could remain connected and make a contribution to the family.

Problems still came up from time to time. One day Irene complained to Clare about Helen's loud music. Clare suggested Irene put it on the agenda and bring it up at their weekly meeting. When she did, Helen complained that Irene had the TV on every afternoon when she came home from school. It was difficult to have friends over and have to listen to soap operas, so she played her music to drown out the TV.

After some lively discussion, Irene agreed to use the small TV in her room in the afternoons, and Helen agreed to keep the volume of her music lowered. Both were relieved to meet their needs without disturbing the other.

The family found that they could deal with the problems that came up and maintain respect for everyone. They were able to talk about their expectations and different styles and work on solutions to problems instead of blaming and arguing. They were fortunate that Irene was willing to talk at their meetings and share her feelings and ideas. They knew that some older people are unaccustomed and unwilling to address issues directly, making it difficult or impossible to resolve issues.

## TURNING ROOMMATES INTO TEAMMATES

Households that materialize instead of those formed with intention (like the Harrises') have the most difficulty with cooperation. Young people who move away from home and form households for the first time often resist structure and advice about how to develop an organized plan of cooperative living. The housemates don't want to be "bossed" now that they no longer live at home; they want to do things their way.

The households that met with the most success were those in which people looked for a living situation that met their needs or formed a household with like-minded people. Whatever the motivation for sharing a household, it's extremely important to have a way of resolving the inevitable conflicts that will occur.

Without that, house members are stuck grinning and bearing a bad situation or doing everything alone. Cooperation is impossible when roommates handle conflict by staying with a friend or avoiding contact completely. If the living arrangement is for a short time, housemates are less motivated to work things out, saying they could put up with the problems for the short time involved.

You can do little to create a team if the others involved don't want to change. For that reason, we recommend you carefully check out the situation first to make sure it will be compatible with your needs. Look for household members who are willing to talk about issues and feelings, have some experience with teamwork, and have a sincere desire to work things out. Since avoiding problems completely is impossible, it is important that potential housemates have both the desire and the tools to work out difficulties. The strategies in previous chapters will help you develop the tools you'll need for cooperative living. Use the pointers below to select a situation that will work for you.

### Tips for Finding Compatible Roommates

1. Look for ads posted where people with interests similar to yours gather.

DEALING WITH ADULT LIVING SITUATIONS

2. Meet and talk with potential roommates to find out more about them. Ask about their interests and daily living habits (especially concerning noise, messiness, pets, and TV), how they like to resolve problems, the actual cost of living in the household, and ideas about sharing those costs. Run a credit check.

3. Find out whose name is on the lease and how people can leave if they aren't satisfied. If your name is on the lease and others leave, you are obligated to find new roommates or cover the costs yourself. Make sure you have a say in accepting or rejecting new roommates.

4. Make sure you are starting with people who want to cooperate and work toward win/win solutions when you check out the new household. Find out if current household members have an established method for resolving conflicts or would be willing to create one.

In the stories below, roommates demonstrated the importance of having both skills and goodwill to help each other deal with issues as they came up. It wasn't always easy to be open and honest, but they found that the more they talked about issues, the easier it was to work out difficulties.

## Sharing Gripes Results in a Game Plan

Valerie thought it was a great idea when Gwen and Seth asked her to share an off-campus apartment with them. She looked forward to being out of the dorm and living on her own. Because she liked Gwen and Seth and was able to talk easily with them, she thought they'd all get along well.

They moved in together and began setting up a household. Their first joint decision was to share food. They planned to shop together and split the bill. The next week at the scheduled time, Gwen said, "Oh, I forgot, I can't go today. They gave me an extra shift at work and I have to get ready. You don't mind if I don't go with you, do you?"

Valerie and Seth both said, "I guess not," and left to do the shopping. At the store they realized they would have to advance Gwen's share of the money for groceries. Even though Gwen paid them back later, it was inconvenient because they didn't have enough money in their accounts and had to make an extra trip to the ATM to deposit Gwen's money. When this happened three weeks in a row, Valerie and Seth felt resentful.

Gwen had resentments, too. She approached Valerie a few days after the shopping was done and said, "I was going to make a sandwich, but all the cheese is gone! What happened to it?"

Valerie replied, "I didn't have any. I think Seth had friends over and made grilled cheese sandwiches. They must have finished it."

Gwen made a face and said, "That's not fair. Seth and his friends eat half the food in the house!"

Valerie replied, "It's true he eats way more than we do. I don't think our food arrangement is working. Seth and I also have some issues about the grocery shopping we haven't shared with you. We need to talk about what's going on."

The three housemates sat down to talk that evening. They all agreed things weren't working as planned and they needed to make some changes. Seth suggested that they share foods like milk, eggs, bread, jam, and condiments, but keep the rest of the food separate.

They tried Seth's idea for a few weeks, but problems continued to arise. They realized this system wasn't working either, so they agreed it would be best for each of them to do their own shopping and keep their food separate. They divided the refrigerator and cabinet space. Each person bought groceries for himself or herself and put them in a designated place. If one cooked and wanted to share, he or she could, but there were no expectations. Except for occasional emergency pilfering that no one seemed to mind, this plan worked best.

Once the food problem was resolved, the three roommates focused on the problems related to cleaning. Originally, everyone agreed to clean together every two weeks. They made a sign-up sheet where each could initial the job selected, then add the date after it was completed. The women noticed they were doing most of the cleaning and decided to talk to Seth.

Valerie began, "Seth, you're never around at cleaning time."

Gwen added, "Yeah, and if you are here, you're being a couch potato. We're doing all the cleaning."

Seth agreed with them and said, "Between work and school, I hardly have any time for myself. I hate to spend it cleaning. I know it has to be done, and I appreciate that you've both been picking up the slack. What I'd like to do is take on the major cleaning at the end of the quarter. I'll scrub the floors, do the windows, move the furniture, vacuum, and stuff like that to make up for my part."

The women agreed, and at the end of the quarter, Seth followed through and did a thorough cleaning. He scrubbed the floors and the bathroom tub and toilet, moved the furniture and vacuumed, washed the windows, and cleaned the oven. It took him an entire weekend, but when he was finished, the apartment sparkled. Everyone was happy with the way they solved the problem and liked the feeling that resulted with them working together.

Sometimes it takes experimenting with different strategies to come up with one that works for everybody. Sometimes a plan works for a while and then it stops working and needs to be reevaluated. It's important to focus on solutions instead of looking for who to blame for the problem. Here's another creative solution to a problem a family of roommates struggled with.

A group of college grads decided to share a household to cut down on expenses and enjoy each other's company. They spent hours working out issues of communal living and tried to reach consensus on every topic. They had a job wheel for daily chores, a home improvement day once every three months for bigger projects, and a weekly potluck so everyone could get together for fun. For the most part, the household ran smoothly, but the one problem they couldn't seem to resolve was the recurring toilet paper shortage.

First, everyone joked and figured the "tissue issue" would take care of itself; then they argued over who bought it last; next they tried taking turns buying; then they tried a chart. Nothing worked. The inability to solve this simple problem was breaking down their team spirit. Arguments erupted that started with "I always . . . ," "You never . . . ," "How come so-and-so doesn't . . . ," and on and on.

After several meetings with no progress, one household member got tired of the debate and said, "Look, everyone give me $5. I'll find out where I can buy a case of toilet paper so we don't have to discuss this again. Our friendships are too important for all this petty bickering." He came home with a case of ninety-six rolls of toilet paper, and that solved the problem for months. His housemates were relieved to find a solution that ended their bickering about what was fair or who was to blame.

In the previous situations, people were able to talk and work out their problems. At times talking doesn't help. Someone may be giving a double message, which means saying one thing and doing something else. When a situation arises where someone continually promises to do a job and doesn't follow through, it's important to "listen" to their actions instead of to their words.

## What to Do When Actions and Words Don't Match

Dan and Gary had been friends in school. They found jobs in the same town and decided to share an apartment. Shortly after they were settled, Dan started to notice he had an uneasy feeling about going home each night. The house was getting messier and messier, and he almost hated to walk in the door. One evening when he went into the kitchen he saw the pile of dishes and pots Gary had left in the sink and he felt his stomach tighten.

He walked into the living room where Gary was watching TV and asked, "Gary, when are you going to get the dishes done? I'd like to make my dinner but there's a pile of dirty dishes in the sink."

Gary responded, "Oh, I forgot. I'll get them done in a little while, after this show is over."

Dan remembered saying things like that to his mother when he was a teenager. He didn't think he was being demanding, but he felt uneasy just the same. Instead of making an issue out of Gary's procrastination, Dan went back into the kitchen, made his dinner, and cleaned up around the piles of dishes. He was thinking about all the other times he had washed all the dishes for Gary, and he felt his anger rise. The next morning before he left for work, Dan noticed the same pile of dishes in the sink.

A few days later Dan was getting his clothes ready to take to the cleaners. Gary walked in and said, "I'm going to the cleaners before work. Just leave your clothes and I'll take them in with mine."

Dan thought, "Maybe I've been unfair and too hard on Gary. He's really a nice guy."

That night when Dan came home, his clothes were where he'd left them. He was angry and asked, "What happened? I thought you were going to the cleaners."

"I ran short of time. I was late for work and decided to do it tomorrow. Don't worry, I'll get it done then."

The next evening Dan again found his clothes where he had left them. Dan promised himself he would never believe what Gary said again. Later that day, Dan discussed the situation with a friend at work who said, "Dan, it looks as if Gary's words don't match his actions. His behavior is the reality, not his promises. You trust his words and end up disappointed. You need to tell him you aren't going to take promises anymore."

That evening the sink was filled with dirty dishes again. Dan asked Gary to turn off the TV because he had something important to say. When he told Gary about the dishes, he heard, "I'm going to do them before I go to bed."

"Gary," Dan said, "I don't take promises any more. Don't tell me, show me."

Gary looked surprised. "What do you mean?"

"I'm more interested in good actions than good intentions. From now on, don't say it. Just do it!" Then Dan walked out of the room without further comment.

Every time Gary started to make a promise about doing something, Dan told him that wasn't acceptable because he wanted action, not words.

One evening Dan came home and found the storage locker had been left open. Gary was eating dinner when Dan came in and said, "The storage locker was left open. I'm concerned our stuff may be taken."

Gary started, "Oh, I . . . ," then paused before he said, "I know. You want action." He got up and locked the cabinet. He'd finally gotten the message.

Dan and Gary demonstrated their intention to work things out. Without the desire to change, nothing would have improved. Had Dan not found a solution, this problem could have escalated into a hostile confrontation resulting in someone's decision to leave.

## HOW TO DEAL WITH AN ABUSIVE SITUATION

In some families, people don't communicate at all, so it is difficult to work anything out. A young woman moved into a large house with fifteen other people to be closer to her boyfriend. For weeks, none of the others realized she was living there, because so many people came and went on different schedules. People pilfered food from each other, slept in a bed if the owner wasn't home without asking permission, and resisted all efforts to plan formal meetings. There were a lot of people with a lot of resentments but no formal process for resolving them. If someone had a complaint, he or she put a hostile or sarcastic note on the refrigerator. People reading the note felt criticized, attacked, and defensive and weren't interested in cooperating.

If you are living with others who refuse to talk, we suggest you look for another place where people are willing to treat each other with respect and talk over differences. You may need to ask an uncooperative or difficult roommate to leave for the same reasons. We emphasize the principles of mutual respect, open communication, and shared decision making, which apply whether you live with a group of people you have just met or with family members.

But what do you do if you are living in a situation that is not only hostile but abusive, and you can't move out because it's your home? Worse yet, the offender refuses to move, and any attempt at conversation results in a blowup or even physical violence. This situation has become more prevalent with many adult children refusing to leave home and/or abusing drugs and alcohol at the same time.

If this situation exists in your house, the first thing you need to do is get active in an Al-Anon group or start reading literature about parents who can't say no, love too much, or are co-dependent. You are now one of those parents, and your attempts to "help" your child by putting up with abuse are only making the situation worse. Perhaps you didn't draw lines and follow through on them when you had the chance, and now the situation has escalated into an ugly and dangerous one. You need outside help either from a counselor, a support group, or the police.

Even though your child is threatening to hurt you or hurt himself or herself, you can still decide what you will do, and do it. In one situation, the mother of a group of addicts who were making her life miserable said, "If you come home without an invitation, I'll call the police and report a trespasser." The kids (in their thirties) didn't believe her, but after she followed through on several occasions, they decided she meant business.

Another parent changed locks while a third bought a rental unit as an investment, moved the adult children to it, and had them evicted by the sheriff when they didn't pay rent. If you think these methods are extreme, you're correct, but the consequences of living with children who refuse to grow up or who insist on abusing drugs and alcohol in your presence are worse.

As we said before, we hope that you will never need this information because you have used the guidelines we've laid out for you as your children were growing up. There is nothing more satisfying than a home that feels safe, friendly, cooperative, and harmonious and people who want to be on the same team. But when safety is an issue, extreme measures may be your only choice.

# CONCLUSION

Recently we received an e-mail from a mom who heard we were revising *Chores without Wars*. Here's what she had to say:

A week ago my husband and I attended Back-to-School night at our son's elementary school. Our kids, nine and twelve, chose to stay home on their own and look out for each other. Before my husband and I left, we reviewed the guidelines with our kids for being home on their own (phone, door), the "emergencies" that warranted a cell phone call to us (blood, barf, fire, quake), and then left for the meeting.

Imagine our delight when we returned home and our twelve-year-old bounded to the door saying, "Mom, we made our lunches, packed our backpacks for tomorrow, did our after-dinner jobs, brushed our teeth, and got ready for bed! Come here, let's have our time together!" Hearing this brought a huge smile to our faces and my husband and I looked at each other, beaming. We knew this was the pay-off for implementing the ideas in this book, one by one, over the years.

We want to let your readers know that although we started reading *Chores without Wars* when our eldest was born, whatever age their children are when they start the book, they should consider the book a gift. If they jump in and try out some of the ideas, in no time their kids can be participating in (or somewhat experienced in) every area of family work—laundry, cleaning, meal prep and clean up, shopping, yard work, meetings, planning social events, handling money, and more. That was our goal when we picked up the book, and we've accomplished it by showing, doing with, guiding from a distance, and following through, following through, and following through.

Teaching our children has been hard work and required continued commitment, but we can't think of a better way to empower our kids and build our family connection. We're excited for the readers who, with this book in hand, will have the tools they need to take the steps towards the goals they have in mind.

The writer of this e-mail (Robin Setchko) uses the ideas in *Chores without Wars* with her clients (she's a licensed family therapist), at her parenting groups (she's a parent educator), with her own family, and in past years, at the camp she directed. Like Robin, we know you can gain a sense of achievement and harmony by involving others in family responsibilities. When you stop struggling to do everything yourself and turn your family into a team, we know how much you'll enjoy watching your children be creative and capable and cooperative.

There is no finish line once you get involved in this process. The more you practice the ideas in *Chores without Wars*, the more you'll realize that you are working on relationships, not just getting work done. The relationship gifts you give your children and other loved ones will keep on giving. As they grow older, they'll be able to help others plan ahead, multitask, believe in themselves, see work as fun, be highly organized, and contribute to the greater good. They will be empowered adults who empower and encourage those around them. They may have very different styles from yours and different applications of the ideas in this book, but when you dig down, you'll find that they are respectful and resourceful and responsible, and they value contribution. Now isn't that worth the effort?

# References

Adler, Alfred. 1958. *What Life Should Mean to You*. New York: Capricorn Books.

———. 1964. *Social Interest*. New York: Capricorn Books.

———. 1964. *Superiority and Social Interest*. Illinois: Northwestern University Press.

———. 1978. *Cooperation between the Sexes*. New York: Anchor Books.

Albert, Linda. 1982. *Coping with Kids*. New York: E. P. Dutton.

Allred, G. Hugh. 1976. *How to Strengthen Your Marriage and Family*. Provo, Utah: Brigham Young University Press.

Ansbacher, Heinz, and Rowena Ansbacher. 1964. *The Individual Psychology of Alfred Adler*. New York: Harper Touchbooks.

Bayard, Robert, and Jean Bayard. 1981. *How to Deal with Your Acting Up Teenager*. San Jose, Calif.: Accord Press.

Beecher, Marguerite, and Willard Beecher. 1966. *Beyond Success and Failure*. New York: Pocket Books.

Bettner, Betty Lou, and Amy Lew. 1992. *Raising Kids Who Can*. New York: Harper Perennial.

Cassel, Pearl, and Raymond J. Corsini. 1990. *Coping with Teenagers in a Democracy*. Toronto: Lugus.

Christiensen, Oscar. 1983. *Adlerian Family Counseling*. Minneapolis, Minn.: Educational Media Corp.

Corsini, Raymond, and Genevieve Painter. 1975. *The Practical Parent*. New York: Harper and Row.

Deline, John. 1981. *Who's Raising the Family?* Madison: Wisconsin Clearing House.

Dinkmeyer, Don, and Rudolf Dreikurs. 1963. *Encouraging Children to Learn: The Encouragement Process*. Englewood Cliffs, NJ: Prentice Hall.

Dinkmeyer, Don, and Gary McKay. 1973. *Raising a Responsible Child*. New York: Simon and Schuster.

———. 1989. *Parents Handbook: Systematic Training for Effective Parenting*. 3rd ed. Circle Pines, Minn.: American Guidance Service.

Dinkmeyer, Don, W. L. Pew, and Don Dinkmeyer Jr. 1979. *Adlerian Counseling and Psychotherapy*. Monterey, Calif.: Brooks/Cole.

Dreikurs, Rudolf. 1971. *Social Equality: The Challenge of Today*. Chicago: Contemporary Books.

——— 1966. *Psychology in the Classroom*. New York: Harper and Row.

Dreikurs, Rudolf, Shirley Gould, and Raymond J. Corsini. 1974. *Family Council*. Chicago: Henry Regnery.

Dreikurs, Rudolf, Bronia Grunwald, and Floyd Pepper. 1971. *Maintaining Sanity in the Classroom*. New York: Harper and Row.

Dreikurs, Rudolf, and V. Soltz. 1964. *Children: The Challenge*. New York: Hawthorn Books.

Dyer, Wayne. 1976. *Your Erroneous Zones*. New York: Avon Books.

Glenn, H. Stephen, and Jane Nelsen. 1988. *Raising Self-Reliant Children in a Self-Indulgent World*. Rocklin, Calif.: Prima.

Glenn, H. Stephen. n.d. *Developing Capable People*. Fair Oaks, Calif.: Sunrise Press. Audiocassette.

———. n.d. *Involving and Motivating People*. Fair Oaks, Calif.: Sunrise Press. Audiocassette.

———. 1989. *Bridging Troubled Waters*. Fair Oaks, Calif.: Sunrise Press. Audiocassette.

———. 1989. *Developing Healthy Self-Esteem.* Fair Oaks, Calif.: Sunrise Press. Videotape.

———. 1989. *Empowering Others: Ten Keys to Affirming and Validating People.* Fair Oaks, Calif.: Sunrise Press. Videotape.

———. 1989. *Introduction to Developing Capable People.* Fair Oaks, Calif.: Sunrise Press. Videotape.

———. 1989. *Six Steps to Developing Responsibility.* Fair Oaks, Calif.: Sunrise Press. Videotape.

———. 1989. *Teachers Who Make a Difference.* Fair Oaks, Calif.: Sunrise Press, 1989. Videotape.

———. 1989. *The Greatest Human Need.* Fair Oaks, Calif.: Sunrise Press. Videotape.

Goldberg, Herb. 1976. *Hazards of Being Male.* New York: New American Library.

Janoe, Ed, and Barbara Janoe. 1973. *About Anger.* Vancouver, Wash.: Arco Press.

———. 1973. *Dealing with Feelings.* Vancouver, Wash.: Arco Press.

Kvols-Reidler, Bill, and Kathy Kvols-Reidler. 1979. *Redirecting Children's Misbehavior.* Boulder, Colo.: R.D.I.C.

Losoney, Lewis. 1980. *You Can Do It.* Englewood Cliffs, N.J.: Prentice Hall.

Lott, Lynn, Riki Intner, and Barbara Mendenhall. 1999. *Do It Yourself Therapy: How to Think, Feel and Act Like a New Person in Just 8 Weeks.* Franklin Lakes, N.J.: Career Press.

Lott, Lynn, Marilyn Kentz, and Dru West. 1983. *To Know Me Is to Love Me.* Santa Rosa, Calif.: Practical Press.

Lott, Lynn, and Jane Nelsen. 1990. *Teaching Parenting Manual.* Fair Oaks, Calif.: Sunrise Press.

Lott, Lynn, and Dru West. 1987. *Together and Liking It.* Santa Rosa, Calif.: Practical Press.

Manaster, Guy J., and Raymond Corsini. 1982. *Individual Psychology.* Itasca, Ill.: F. E. Peacock.

Nelsen, Jane. n.d. *Positive Discipline.* Fair Oaks, Calif.: Sunrise Press. Audiocassette.

———. 1987. *Positive Discipline.* New York: Ballantine Books.

———. 1988. *Positive Discipline*. Fair Oaks, Calif.: Sunrise Press. Videotape.

———. 1988. *Positive Discipline Study Guide*. Fair Oaks, Calif.: Sunrise Press.

———. 1988. *Understanding: Eliminating Stress and Finding Serenity in Life and Relationships*. Rocklin, Calif.: Prima.

Nelsen, Jane, Cheryl Erwin, and Carol Delzer. 1994. *Positive Discipline for Single Parents*. Rocklin, Calif.: Prima.

Nelsen, Jane, and H. Stephen Glenn. 1991. *Time Out: Abuses and Effective Uses*. Fair Oaks, Calif.: Sunrise Press.

Nelsen, Jane, Riki Intner, and Lynn Lott. 1996. *Positive Discipline for Parenting in Recovery*. Rocklin, Calif.: Prima.

Nelsen, Jane, and Lynn Lott. 1994. *Positive Discipline for Teenagers*. Rocklin, Calif.: Prima.

Nelsen, Jane, Lynn Lott, and H. Stephen Glenn. 1997. *Positive Discipline in the Classroom*. Rocklin, Calif.: Prima.

———. 1993. *Positive Discipline A–Z*. Rocklin, Calif.: Prima.

Pew, W. L., and J. Terner. 1978. *Courage to Be Imperfect*. New York: Hawthorn Books.

Smith, Manuel J. 1975. *When I Say No I Feel Guilty*. New York: Dial Press.

Walton, F. X. 1994. *Winning Teenagers Over*. Columbia, S.C.: Adlerian Child Care Books.

# INDEX

# About the Authors

**Lynn Lott, M.A., M.F.T.,** holds two master's degrees in counseling and psychology and is lovingly called the female Dr. Phil by her clients and friends. She is coauthor of several self-help books, including *Positive Discipline A–Z* (with Jane Nelsen and H. Stephen Glenn), *Positive Discipline for Teenagers* (with Jane Nelsen), *Positive Discipline for Parenting in Recovery* (with Jane Nelsen and Riki Intner), *Positive Discipline in the Classroom* (with Jane Nelsen and H. Stephen Glenn), *Do It Yourself Therapy* (with Riki Intner and Barbara Mendenhall), and most recently her book written with novelist Nancy Pickard, *Seven Steps on the Writer's Path*. She has also recently published a card set called *Madame Dora's Fortune-Telling Cards*. In 2005, Lynn will be publishing *Pup Parenting* (coauthored with Jane Nelsen and Therry Jay).

Lynn, a well-known and busy family therapist, has taught parenting since 1969, trained family therapists, taught courses at Sonoma State University, traveled the United States and Canada to present workshops for parents, teachers, and therapists, and founded and directed the Family Education Centers of Sonoma County. She is a Diplomate in the North American Society of Adlerian Psychology. Lynn is as comfortable on a radio or TV talk show as she is skiing down the black diamond runs in the winter. She is the mother of two and stepmother of two, and now has the joy of revisiting family work with her grandson Zachary. She divides her time between California and Florida with husband Hal Penny and her mini schnauzer Magic.

**Riki Intner, M.A., M.F.T.,** is a marriage and family therapist in private practice for over twenty years in Santa Rosa and San Francisco, California. She works with couples, individuals, and families and also conducts workshops and training sessions at conferences, schools, businesses, and community events. She is a Diplomate in Adlerian Psychology. Riki has served on the boards of the North American Society of Adlerian Psychology and the Rotary Club of Fisherman's Wharf–San Francisco, of which she was president. She has served her Rotary District 5150 as an assistant governor.

Riki's articles appear in various publications and she has been interviewed on radio many times. She is the coauthor of several self-help books, including *Positive Discipline for Parenting in Recovery* (with Jane Nelsen and Lynn Lott), *Do It Yourself Therapy* (with Lynn Lott and Barbara Mendenhall), and the soon to be released *Caregiving from the Heart: Tales of Inspiration.* She lives in San Francisco with her husband after raising three children who now have children of their own using the principles of family work.